T0326251

EASY LESSONS IN ECONOMICS

EASY LESSONS

IN

ECONOMICS

By

E. E. HOUSELEY, B.A., B.Sc. [Econ.]

Late Derby Scholar and History Exhibitioner of London University
Headmaster of the Cheetham Senior School, Manchester
Formerly Senior English and History Master at
the Wandsworth S.W. Secondary School

CAMBRIDGE

AT THE UNIVERSITY PRESS

1933

CAMBRIDGE
UNIVERSITY PRESS

University Printing House, Cambridge CB2 8BS, United Kingdom

Cambridge University Press is part of the University of Cambridge.

It furthers the University's mission by disseminating knowledge in the pursuit of
education, learning and research at the highest international levels of excellence.

www.cambridge.org
Information on this title: www.cambridge.org/9781316606896

© Cambridge University Press 1933

First published 1933
First paperback edition 2016

A catalogue record for this publication is available from the British Library

ISBN 978-1-316-60689-6 Paperback

Cambridge University Press has no responsibility for the persistence or accuracy
of URLs for external or third-party internet websites referred to in this publication,
and does not guarantee that any content on such websites is, or will remain,
accurate or appropriate.

PREFACE

These simple lessons are based on a course which seemed successful when given to pupils of ordinary ability during their last two terms in a reorganized senior school. During the previous term lessons inspired by the "Real Life Geography" of Dr L. Dudley Stamp were given. Beyond this all that was assumed was the usual knowledge of History and Arithmetic possessed by these young people. It was part of their training to make a fuller use of works of reference and certain sections of the newspapers than is perhaps usual. The personal observations of the scholars were worked into the lessons easily and naturally.

The value of the subject to school-leavers to prepare them for getting a living, spending money wisely, and living a life of social worth, is generally admitted. It is hoped that this course of lessons will not be found too academic in type for young economists: the aim, at any rate, was to be practical throughout.

The stress laid in the written version on the word Economics did not appear at first in the lessons. Terminology of that kind was steadily regarded by the author as a delusion and a snare; but the pupils dragged it forth: they undoubtedly liked to think that they were beginning a new subject with a name like that.

The author desires to thank his colleagues, Mr Lucas, B.Sc. (Econ.) and Mr McKinley, for their assistance; and also the authors, publishers, and editors who have kindly permitted a few short extracts from copyright matter to be included in these lessons. The books thus used happened to be in the school library, and have been of great service. The author ventures to recommend them very strongly to those teachers who are fortunate enough to be making additions to their school libraries.

E. E. H.

August 1932

CONTENTS

CHAPTER I

BIG BUSINESS

Amid whirring machines and tall smoking chimneys it is not easy to picture the work of smiths, carpenters, and potters of bygone ages. Yet it was not until the nineteenth century that machines defeated hand labourers in all the main industries. Then appeared the factories, with dull narrow streets of badly-built houses for the workers. Factory life meant town life. Throughout the nineteenth century the growth of the industrial centres continued. The busy cities of the Victorian age were often very ugly; but the wages paid by the employers in towns were much higher than those offered by farmers, and many of the best boys and girls left the villages.

The saddest example of this urban drift, as it is sometimes called, may be found in a story written by H. G. Wells, *The Food of the Gods, and How it came to Earth.* There we read of Caddles, of the village of Cheasing Eyebright. Like the huge wasps and the giant rats in the story, he ate of the wonderful food and became a mighty man. So bulky was he after a time that he was withdrawn from attendance at school, since the other children made fun of the young man-mountain.

Later he worked in a chalk-pit. By means of a great windlass he hauled empty trucks from the siding up the railway lines, dug his chalk, loaded it, and finally himself ran his rolling stock where it was required.

He was able to work the entire quarry single-handed, and for a long time he seemed quite satisfied with his job.

He had become a very powerful giant, and thus did not find his work too difficult. But Caddles wished to understand things. It was when he became puzzled and discontented that his troubles began.

"Why should I work in this pit, day after day?" he asked. At length he left his job at the quarry, and sought the answer to his questions in London.

Picture him now amid the traffic of the great city, gazing vacantly at omnibuses, cars, trams, carts, trolleys, cyclists, and an astonished crowd of people. From the shops customers came and stared at him, workmen gathered round him, little boys and loafers, shopping women and nursemaids, could not leave him in peace. At length he spoke to them. "I don't understand it," he said. His brows were knit. "Why do you exist, you swarming little people?" he asked. "What are you all doing? What are you all for?"

"He knew nothing of money," writes Mr Wells, "this monstrous simpleton, nothing of trade, nothing of the social fabric of the little people." "I didn't know there were such places as this," he cried again and again to the crowd. "What are all you people doing with yourselves? What's it all for? And where do *I* come in?"

Caddles stood in Piccadilly Circus between eleven and twelve at night, and watched the ladies in their cars, the people emerging from the restaurants, and ragged misery sneaking along the gutter. Let us remind ourselves that our giant knew nothing of trade and money. Standing at his corner he peered at the people and asked them questions, but he never found the key to the maze.

The knowledge for which poor Caddles at length sacrificed his life is to be found in this little book. No one who takes the trouble to study Economics need ever worry a busy city crowd by questions about work and wages. It is the business of those who teach Economics to supply answers of the kind required by Caddles. Some people call Economics the science of the endeavour to satisfy human want. It is the science of business, the study of mankind in the ordinary affairs of life.

This does not mean that the economist—and particularly the young economist—must be a farmer, a banker, an engineer, a shopkeeper and a chemist all rolled into one. His job is not to study the whole of the matter. What are the wants of man, and how does he set about supplying them? How much is an article worth, and what makes it worth that amount? The economist tries to find answers to questions such as these. He is concerned with prices, markets, goods, work, money, and wages. If a man is at work, he wants to know why. If a man is not at work he again wants to know why.

What do our modern industrial cities look like through the glasses of the economist? Here we can deal directly with some of the problems which puzzled Caddles. The products of every land and clime are to be found in the big shops. The sum total of human knowledge is there, but only for those who have eyes to see. Every purchaser obtains material for thought as well as for enjoyment, or, as we say, for consumption. Before the smoker lights a cigarette he may sometimes like to think through how many busy hands the tobacco has already passed. Every automobile is an advertisement of the vast importance of the oils of far-away lands. The fur coats displayed for sale remind us that Economics must take note of useful animals. For behind the shop window we see the furry creatures of the woods, with a goodly sprinkling of friendly rabbits darting hither and thither. The rubber planter overseas is one of the pillars of the modern city. Thus does the economist try to read the riddle of the market-place.

The man for whom Caddles was looking in vain was Burning Daylight, who could have answered all his questions. Burning Daylight is a hero of Jack London, and is said to have earned his curious name by routing his Arctic comrades out of their blankets with the shout that daylight was burning. His feats as a pioneer among the miners on the Yukon delight all who love tales of adventure.

Burning Daylight, however, understood not only dogs and trails, but also the way in which the parts of a modern city are fitted together.

It is, after all, the city which is the great stage of commerce. Knowledge of the dormitory suburbs, the route to work, the favourite shops, and places of amusement, is not enough. What should be known is the whole framework, the complex build of a trading town. The stage is the whole city, and it is a born town-planner who can explain it to us.

"Daylight had vision," writes Jack London. That

is why, when he left Circle City to follow the trail to Stewart, he spoke of staking town sites, organizing trading companies, and starting banks in those lonely wastes. When he first mentioned banks and stock exchanges in Alaska, his companions exploded with mirth. Still, he persisted in his notions. On the woody, snow-covered plain he saw in imagination a mining city; he had an eye for steam-boat landings, and locations for saw-mills and warehouses.

At length it came—the gold metropolis on the Yukon. Burning Daylight's great city of Ophir arose on the vast moose-pastures. His engines built a reservoir eighty miles from the settlement, and a huge wooden conduit carried the water from the watershed across country to Ophir. We read how the mining town developed step by step. We see, for example, machinery being used more and more in the hunt for gold. Electric power plants are installed, and the workings are lighted, as well as run, by electricity. The cabins of the miners are then erected, saw-mills are built, and finally the banks of which Daylight had spoken actually appear. Caddles of Cheasing Eyebright would have been puzzled in Ophir as well as in London. When the shrill whistles called hundreds of labourers to work he would have been startled. Had the glare of the arc-lamps revealed to him this busy northern hive of industry, he would again have asked helplessly, "What does it all mean?"

At a later date Burning Daylight left the Northern city he had built, and descended upon San Francisco. There he proceeded to solve problem after problem connected with the life of a great city. He was fas-

cinated by the activities of the great captains of industry, and became known himself throughout America
as a great financier.

The greatest scheme of Daylight is fully explained
by Jack London. Oakland was near San Francisco,
and was much more attractive, for residential purposes,
than the greater city. However, the transport system
between the two was very bad. A fine scheme of
ferries with modern boats was planned. A huge pier
was to be constructed. "I will build electric roads,"
said Daylight, "and the land of Oakland will then
become very valuable; then fine houses will soon
appear. Here will be a system of docks suitable for
ocean steamers. Connected with them will be the
freight cars of three great railways. What will follow?
Why, factories! Factory sites will then be needed.
Factories mean tens of thousands of working men and
their families. That means more houses and more
land. A growing population will need more stores,
more banks, more places of amusement, more everything." This town-planner understood Economics.

"Here are all the material advantages," he said,
"for a great metropolis. Do you want to land your
tea and silk from Asia, and ship it straight East? Here
are the docks for your steamers, and here are the rail-
roads. Do you want factories from which you can ship
direct by land or water? Here's the site, and here's
the modern up-to-date city, with the latest improvements for yourselves and your workmen to live in."

"Then there's the water," he went on, and showed
how a good water system would be provided. "Look
at it. Just look at it," said Burning Daylight. "You

could never find a finer site for a great city. Twenty years from now there'll be a million people on this side of the bay."

To most of us a city is like a jig-saw puzzle. It is a great gift to be able to fit the parts together in orderly

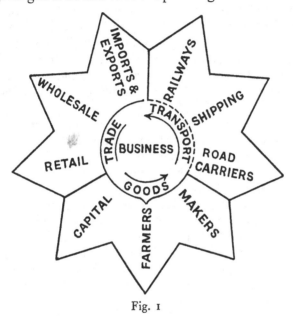

Fig. 1

fashion in our minds; it is wonderful to be able to guess usefully what a city will be like at some time in the future. All this is very important to us because we have become a race of city dwellers. These are the people whom the economist studies in the ordinary business of life, although he does not forget the farmer, the miner, and the fisherman.

But for a long time our chief national business has been shopkeeping. In our shops the finished products of industry are placed upon the counter. The pictures of John Bull to which we have grown accustomed represent a prosperous farmer whose favourite recreation would appear to be hunting; but the ordinary Englishman to-day goes forth to make, to buy, and to sell. During the "rush hour," crowds of men and women, boys and girls, hurry from their dormitories in the suburbs to the railway or car, and onwards to factory or market. We sometimes call the crowds of business people "daily breaders."

The economic activities of all these workers are to be studied to some extent. What do they make? How do they help one another? Where do they show their skill? What mistakes are they likely to make?

It is not too difficult for us. Think of the blunders made by the traders in the age of Walpole who are said to have planned to supply tropical countries with warming-pans. This was a first-class error in the study of the wants of man. We read in the same age of a company being formed to import jackasses from Spain, "as if," someone said, "we had not plainly jackasses enough already." One adventurer in those times asked for £1,000,000 to make a wheel for perpetual motion; and someone at some time must undoubtedly have carried coals to the Newcastle market.

Trade means buying and selling. A boom is a loud hollow sound, a sort of roar. The rush of a ship produces the sound of booming water. When there is a sudden and great demand for goods, there is said to be a trade boom. "The boom was something wonderful," writes Mark Twain, "everybody bought, everybody sold."

A slump, on the contrary, means that the boom has finished. There is a sudden fall in the price of goods, stocks, and shares. Slump is a dismal word, indeed; it attempts to imitate the cheerless sinking of a body in mud or snow.

It is a curious thing that every period of from seven to ten years seems to include a trade boom followed by a trade slump. When people want to know why this is, they turn to the subject of Economics for an answer. As yet, however, this particular answer is not very clear.

To us all business means serious work; it is our care and concern. A man who means business is in earnest; a man on business comes with a definite purpose. It is during business hours that the shop or office is open; and the business end of a tin tack is its point.

The economist studies this business activity. He guides the learner to the countryside among the miners and the farmers. He shows the uses of the great machines of industry. He points to the goods produced by means of these agents; and tracks them to their markets, as they are transported by road, rail, sea, or air. Then comes the actual riddle of the market-place, and the buying and selling that we know in our shops. Wealth is what costs something. A man's wealth is the money value of his possessions. The economist explains as well as he can how desirable things are produced and then shared. He shows what is the prey of the hunter, and why and how it must be

chased. Then when victory is gained, the sharing of
the spoils is still difficult to understand.

This reference to hunting reminds us that the study
of mankind in the ordinary affairs of life, may include
the services rendered by animals. We may fairly end
our first chapter by an easy little economic excursion
of this kind. The producers of fur coats have already
been mentioned and sympathized with. Young people
have always taken the keenest interest in stories about
hunting for trade in order to get marketable skins and
hides. The export of ivory was for many years a considerable item from West Africa. Ivory, however, is
now so cheap that there is not the same inducement
to export it. One feels pleased that the elephants may
therefore breathe more freely. Unfortunately elephant
meat commands a high price in the local markets of
the Gold Coast; and the steady and heavy toll of elephants proceeds. As the young and human economist
broods upon the uncertain fates of the domesticated
animals, it may be found that genuine economic reason-
ing is going on. Here are some typical first economic
exercises of this kind.

A lady recently commenced her lessons on Economics
by talking about the supply of fat cattle in relation to
cooking. She explained that housewives now find that
big joints of meat cannot be cooked in the small ovens
of labour-saving flats. When butchers cannot sell these
large joints they refuse to buy from farmers the heavier
types of cattle. Farmers then try to breed cattle which
will not have such large joints as were usual some years
ago.

If the annual license paid for dogs were doubled,

how would the Tail-waggers League be affected? What would happen if no license at all had to be obtained? Ought a farmer to be allowed a sheepdog free? All these are economic questions. What we notice with regard to animals is a survival of the most useful at any particular time. A writer in the *Manchester Guardian* recently pointed out that through the heavy taxation of the times, many hunting packs in different parts of the country are being disbanded. The hounds in these conditions become unemployed dogs, and foxes and stags rejoice. The same writer also noted that in the streets of our towns cart-horses are getting fewer and fewer as cars of various kinds replace them. We are all able to notice changes like these. The tram-horse and fire-brigade horse have gone for ever, and the heavy dray-horse is now rarely seen. In the country the farmers are no longer engaged in breeding such horses; hay and corn are not being grown for them, and their stables and harness are no longer made. All these are economic changes.

Will the race-horse survive? Both rich and poor seem to value very highly the luxury of horse-racing. Will the racing dog oust the horse, or will both exist together?

The cavalry charger is disappearing with the advance of mechanical warfare, and still another of our old friends is preparing to depart. "What is happening," asked the same sympathetic writer, "to the kindly plough-horse, with his shaggy ankles?" How can he continue to exist in these days of motor tractors? When our present generation of spinster ladies with limited means and ample leisure dies out, what modern young business women will bother to carry round a Pekingese ? Cats, on the other hand, will probably live on, as they have lived already through the centuries. If neglected in the country, they can soon adapt themselves to a life of the wilds and open spaces. If taxed in the towns, they can at any time stray from their homes. They are much more skilful than dogs in their standing feud with motor cars. More than this—in more than one city they are civic functionaries, paid for by the corporation "to clear the town of rats." To-day in Berlin the Pied Piper's work is done just as efficiently by the corporation cats. They alone of all animals can cope with the filth of civilization, and can keep themselves spotless and in perfect health.

Such truths are revealed by an economic inquiry in the realm of the animals.

QUESTIONS AND EXERCISES

1. Write a letter explaining the meaning of Economics, so that a friend who is not learning the subject may know something about it.

2. Show how a large number of workers must co-operate before an orange can be brought from Spain to an English shop.

3. Draw a plan of that part of your city which seems to you most important to business; and give reasons for your choice.

4. Would you rather learn to make (a) harness for horses, or (b) some part of a car? Which occupation is likely to provide surer employment in the future?

5. Select some article—*e.g.* a fountain pen, a pair of boots, or a ready-made garment—for an imaginary sale, and state briefly the chief points with regard to it that you would try to impress upon a possible customer. Show how you could make your points clear.

6. What are the chief disadvantages of tramways?

Write a few lines on the use of each of the following means of transport: (*a*) charabancs, (*b*) taxi-cabs, (*c*) motor omnibuses, (*d*) private cars.

7. Would you prefer in later life to work in the city or in the country? Why? If you could choose for yourself, what job would you select? Why?

CHAPTER II

SHOPS, TRADE, AND OCCUPATIONS

In one form or another the flesh, skins, tusks or feathers of many birds and beasts arrive in shops. A talk about general shopkeeping, however, should precede an inquiry into the meat, leather, and luxury trades. This will lead us well into the riddles of the market-place. In these days girls, as well as boys, must talk shop. At some time or other most young ladies have imagined themselves to be in charge of some kind of flourishing retail establishment. Their young gentlemen friends at these periods have generally been brooding deeply on the problems arising out of the locomotion of mechanical toys

Enterprising business houses engaged in the manufacture of sweets and soaps, sometimes present schools with model shops, of which the stock-in-trade consists of a brave array of empty tins. And we were a nation of shopkeepers even before this!

Every schoolgirl—yes, and every schoolboy—has paid many a visit to the local merchant or shopkeeper. This local general shop may be turned for us into a sort of commercial school, where the subjects taught are chiefly business, sales, markets, supply and demand, and getting a living. These problems as presented by a small general shopkeeper may seem very simple, but really they are very hard indeed to understand. Yet every young scholar will agree that they must be faced. At one early stage a baby boy or girl gets the idea that the job of walking has simply got to be done; and it is attacked with tremendous pluck. In this book, we are concerned with young people who have grasped the truth that the riddle of the market-place has simply got to be solved. There is the challenge! In the work at the very commencement children who live at a shop will get the best start. A few things, however, we all know.

When goods are bought or sold in large quantities the trade is said to be wholesale. The term "market" does not always mean a particular place; but it does always refer to something which is being bought and sold. Traders may properly talk about a world market for tea or iron, because people all over the world are bidding against one another for these things. Sellers in retail markets are buyers in wholesale markets. Before any small shopkeeper buys in the wholesale market he must know what his customers want. And he must know exactly! It is quite easy for a shopkeeper to fill his shop with honest wares, which are just a little too dear for his customers. If there is much unemployment around a local merchant's shop, he will often, very unwillingly, be compelled to buy cheaper goods of poorer quality from the wholesaler.

The retail trader, then, buys goods wholesale, and then sells them in small parcels or as single articles. The job of the retailer is to find out what his customers want, and then to buy such goods from the wholesaler, and keep them in stock. The wholesale merchant buys large quantities of goods from the manufacturer, and then sells them to the retailer in smaller quantities. We buy from our local grocer a pound of tea; he buys from

the wholesale merchant what his customers are likely
to require; the wholesale buyer of tea buys by the ton.
We are not part of his tea market at all; neither is our
local shopkeeper.

From our retailer, however, we can always obtain
our goods at once; we can get exactly what we happen
to want, and he is often able to deliver them soon after
the order is given. If we have any complaints to make
with regard to the goods supplied, he will probably
help to put the matter right.

But our local trader is not playing at shop: he is, on
the contrary, working hard at shop. Commerce is not
a game for him. Perhaps he opened the establishment
for the first time. What an anxious period that would
be! Perhaps he had to seek a loan from a local bank
at that time. Before he knew his customers as well as
he does now, their wants could not be catered for so
well. This means that some articles which they required he had not bought for them; on the other hand,
he had purchased from the wholesaler a stock of things
for which there was no sale whatever. His rent was perhaps very heavy, and all sorts of expenses had to be
incurred in fitting up his shop.

Business men have none of the first careless rapture
of little girls playing at shop. They seem, in one way
or another, to grumble a great deal. In the country
districts the farmers are just the same: they generally
admit that at some time in the past they have made
profits, but the good times always seem to have gone.

What business worries can a small shopkeeper
have? His shop may seem to be well equipped, his
customers seem very numerous and very loyal; yet he

always seems troubled about many things. As he prepares his useful advertisements for the local newspaper or the cinema screen, or as he tastefully dresses his shop window, perhaps he will tell us of them.

Well, he has to face the competition of many rivals. There is, for example, the pedlar of his wares, the

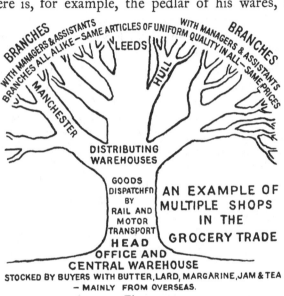

BRANCHES WITH MANAGERS & ASSISTANTS ALL ALIKE — SAME ARTICLES OF UNIFORM QUALITY WITH MANAGERS & ASSISTANTS IN ALL — SAME PRICES BRANCHES

LEEDS

HULL

MANCHESTER

DISTRIBUTING WAREHOUSES

GOODS DISPATCHED BY RAIL AND MOTOR TRANSPORT

HEAD OFFICE AND CENTRAL WAREHOUSE
STOCKED BY BUYERS WITH BUTTER, LARD, MARGARINE, JAM & TEA
— MAINLY FROM OVERSEAS.

AN EXAMPLE OF MULTIPLE SHOPS IN THE GROCERY TRADE

Fig. 2

house-to-house canvasser. Not far away is a public market-place where many of the goods in his shop can be bought at rather cheaper rates. The co-operative store is in the same business. Is that all?

No! for the multiple shop system has come to stay. These shops are all very much alike, and, as we describe them, every scholar will probably be able to think of

one. As a rule, they supply a few articles only, like
butter, tea, lard, bacon, cheese and honey, but they are
retail shops all the same. They are managed from a
central office in some large town. Now, can these shops
be named?

There is a further dragon in the path, in the shape
of the great departmental store. We can all think of
one of these huge stores which combine, in one great
building, department after department, each retailing
a different group of goods. And in addition to all these
rivals of our friend, the small shopkeeper, there is another danger; for there are men who write books on
trade in which they openly ask the following question:
"Is the retail trader absolutely necessary?"

There is indeed a great difference between playing
and working at shop.

Many of the people living near a school do work
which helps to supply the shopkeeper with his goods.
An inquiry may be started at any time by young people
with regard to the subject, and the results of the research work may be usefully set in a notebook and
learned. Sometimes the information thus obtained is
found to be very interesting: an acrobat or a lion-tamer
may be discovered; there may be policemen, soldiers,
sailors, and airmen in the vicinity. The palates of a
small number of workers are so fine that they are able
to taste different kinds of tea and blend them for our
use; we may thus find a tea-taster among us.

A local directory will tell us much of the occupations
of people who may be richer or poorer than ourselves.
In one part of a city we may notice that the houses seem
rather large and the gardens more extensive and beauti-

ful. People in the same area tend to imitate one another in what we call their standard of life. Their food, drink, furniture, and clothes reach what we may call the same standard or quality or class. It is what this group of people have to spend which enables them to enjoy the pleasures of a particular standard of living. Well, what do they do to earn their desirable incomes? The local directory will tell us quite a lot about them. We may add a little from one source or another. In one street which we have noticed, the directory may inform us that a dental surgeon occupies the corner house. We pass on quickly. The next house is that of a commercial traveller. He is not often at home, for his work is to seek customers for cotton goods in the countries along the Mediterranean coast of North Africa. This man spent years in studying foreign languages; he has special knowledge of the needs of the merchants in his foreign markets, and also of the work done in the factories of his firm. His neighbours are a journalist, and a civil servant who holds a responsible position in the Post Office. Next comes the manager of a local bank, who lives near an engineer. The latter can tell many interesting stories of life abroad, for he has helped to build well-known bridges in India and Egypt. He himself is in charge of outside constructional work, but not far away resides another servant of his famous firm, whose work is chiefly to prepare plans in the office at headquarters. On the other side of the road lives a busy builder, and, quite suitably, near at hand is the home of a prosperous painter and decorator. No wonder we noticed an attractive colour scheme at his house! Other occupants of houses in this street are a coal merchant, a retired sea captain, and a well-known professional golfer. The club to which the latter is attached is a few miles away and is very fashionable and flourishing: our "professional" travels to and from it in his car. An official in an insurance company and a manufacturer of batteries for wireless sets also live near.

Then there are advertisements to tell us of the world's work. Our friend the journalist helps to produce them for us, and a useful collection may be made from the morning and evening newspapers in any public reading-room. Young people are naturally most interested in the demands thus revealed for junior office and railway servants. We like to think of those openings for boys and girls which will provide a career for talent and industry; and young gardeners, planters, carpenters, policemen, and domestic servants should, like the rest of us, step forth gaily into the great adventure of getting a living, and greet the unseen with a cheer!

What worlds for boys and girls to conquer are revealed by a collection of these advertisements! Salesmen are required. There are vacancies for well-educated young ladies as correspondence clerks and private secretaries. Girl clerks, typists, and stenographers are advertised for very frequently. Some most attractive vacancies may lead a boy to the coveted position of manager of a mill, or to the clever work of a designer for a textile firm, or to the well-paid job of a buyer of raw materials or goods in the wholesale market. A designer must be a youth of very original ideas.

An expert buyer, *e.g.* in cotton, must sometimes be

prepared to go to America or Egypt to judge the quality of the raw material. There are numerous vacancies for routine workers, *e.g.* for book-keepers and cashiers. One advertisement may later lead a boy to the position of an architect; if he answers another he may rise to the work of controlling the victualling of a big steamship.

How many sums does a boy work dealing with stocks and shares? There are certain positions advertised which may lead such a scholar to the Stock Exchange itself! One may find adventure in farming and forestry abroad; another may use his knowledge of chemistry in dyeworks or shops at home or overseas. A boy may soon find himself managing river or coastwise steam craft in West Africa, or he may be trained for engineering work in the far East. There is romance in commerce and industry!

Yet all these different workers must in some strange way be linked together: it must be team-work really. What is the key to the connection of all these different tasks?

It is the purpose of this little book to attempt to reveal it to some extent. No one understands it altogether. Here is an example of the exercises we shall be working together. Consider all the workers we know. Can we group them in similar classes? How far does the following attempt cover the whole field?

There are workers like fishermen and farmers, who obtain from land or water for the markets things which grow, like corn, rubber, and seals. Then there is another group which extracts for our use goods like coal, salt, and diamonds. Other workers make up these things into other forms through the help of machines in factories: they manufacture the raw materials into goods for which there is a need or demand. Others transport these commodities to where they are required for use. Then there are the people who buy or sell them. Domestic servants, teachers, actors, policemen,

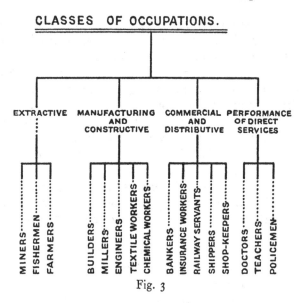

Fig. 3

and soldiers are not included in any of these groups: they render direct services to their fellows. Can anyone think of a better arrangement or grouping of workers? If so, let us have it.

Here is another example of the exercises which we are about to work together. Let us visit once more our local retail shopkeeper and ask him if he can explain why trade is bad at some particular time. There may be what is called a trade depression, and he will feel bound to have some sort of explanation of it.

"Well," he may say, "houses are dear, and all the people near here are buying their houses; so they have not much to spend on other things."

If food were dear throughout the country, this might be another useful explanation. A Manchester shop-keeper might say, "There has been a bad cotton harvest in America; that means dear cotton for us. There is, then, a trade depression in cotton, and that is passed on to other trades. Some of my customers are cotton-spinners, and now they are unemployed. How can these men spend money in my shop? I have to share in the cotton trade depression."

All this may be partly true. No one really understands the whole truth about the causes of bad trade. Another business man—a tailor, for example—might say: "People now, before they make things, have to guess in advance what their customers will want. Well, they sometimes guess wrongly, and make things which nobody wants, or they make more than people need. It is a sure thing that clothes will be required; but manufacturers have to guess in advance what stocks of cloth should be made; and if they guess wrongly, trade will be bad. They will be unable to sell their goods."

If everyone guesses or estimates the wants of others correctly, we can all get many things almost as soon as we want them, instead of having to wait for them to be made.

Our services have to be exchanged. A man makes

a suit of clothes, and in one way or another he must receive food, shelter, and other desirable things through the services of others. We are all parts of a great productive machine.

At school the idea of competition is well understood. What of the race? What of the prize? If races and prizes went, much would go with them. But at school there is co-operation, too. The team battles for all.

We shall find much of this mutual co-operation in trade. All workers form a sort of co-operation for mutual service. "You do this. I will do that. Then we will exchange." That is the understanding in industry and commerce. But no one can say in advance exactly what others will need when the work is done. Glittering prizes are to be won by those among us who know all there is to be known about the wants of others.

QUESTIONS AND EXERCISES

1. Explain what is meant by (*a*) retail trade, (*b*) wholesale trade, (*c*) home trade, (*d*) foreign trade.

2. Write down the names of ten different occupations, and say in each case to what group the worker belongs.

3. What shops do we always find in the main shopping streets? Is a butcher's shop likely to be successful in a side street?

4. Describe some different types of businesses to be found in the retail trade.

5. What advantages does a successful tradesman hope to gain by opening branch shops?

6. Name as many multiple shops as you can, and say what goods are offered for sale in them. Could shops of this kind compete with the greengrocery trade?

7. Why are there great differences in the following businesses with regard to rapidity of turnover of stock?

> (*a*) A retail fishmonger's.
>
> (*b*) A baker's.
>
> (*c*) A milliner's.
>
> (*d*) An ironmonger's.

CHAPTER III

GOODS

When Robinson Crusoe wanted a plough, he had first
to save a store of food to live on while he made it.
Robinson Crusoe worked entirely for himself; when
he toiled he considered only his own wants. He just
managed to live, but his labour assisted no one else.
"I made me a suit of clothes," he writes, "wholly
of skins....I must not mind to acknowledge that they
were wretchedly made; for if I was a bad carpenter, I
was a worse tailor." He ploughed a lonely furrow.
Alone he sowed and reaped; the harvest was his alone.
Only poor food and scanty clothing did he possess
after all his efforts.

Thinking about people like Robinson Crusoe helps
us, no doubt; but even if our wants are so very simple
that they do not differ much from his, it is very clear
that they are not satisfied in the same way.

In *The Admirable Crichton*, a play by Sir J. M.
Barrie, Lord Loam and his house-party leave Mayfair
for a yachting cruise on "The Bluebell." Crichton,
the butler, did not seem very important in London;
but when "The Bluebell" became a mass of floating
wreckage in the Pacific Ocean, he stood forth as a
leader of men.

Imagine the shipwrecked party, then, marooned
on a desert island. Around them are lagoons, rocks,
palm trees, and a sea of bamboo; but there are no
railways, shops, warehouses, or factories. Of course

these unfortunate pleasure-seekers have not become, through the wreck, primitive men and women: unlike the genuine natives of the Pacific Islands, they possess many goods which they have saved from the ship, and their wants are simply immense.

They find it difficult to obtain the service even of fire. "I tried for hours," said Lord Loam, "to make a fire. The authors say that when wrecked on an island you can obtain a light by rubbing two pieces of stick together. The liars!"

At the very moment when the nobleman was speaking, the Admirable Crichton was actually making a fire; but not by rubbing two sticks together. He had placed dry grass beneath some sticks, had made a lens from the glasses of two watches with a little water between them, and was trying to focus the sun's rays upon them. After one failure the grass took fire.

There was, however, no coal in the jungle. How much more complicated are our arrangements in England for obtaining fuel and igniting it! We might consider in some detail the story of the match which we think essential, or the paper and wood as well as the coal.

We regard coal as wealth because it is one of the things which we are able to use and enjoy, and it can be exchanged for other desirable goods. The forces of nature and human effort co-operate to produce it on our markets. Assuming that coal has been dis-covered in the earth and that a shaft has been sunk, we see our first helper hacking coal in an underground seam. Away it goes on a truck to the foot of the shaft, when winders and carters move it to the railway. Coal merchants now come into the story, and railway men transport the fuel to the coal market. Other carters are now required to throw our fuel into the cellars of the city, and finally other useful workers must arrange it on a domestic or an industrial fire.

It is very well, too, to talk glibly about railways and simply to take passing note of their existence and use, but there is neither rolling stock, iron road, nor skilled transport labour on a desert island. What must be done before these desirable modern means of transport and communication can be introduced among bamboos and palms?

Nature must supply iron and coal, and human genius must discover how to apply the powers of steam, and also the processes by which steel is produced. Recent advances have led workers of this type to make great use of the oils supplied by nature, and to harness electricity in the service of man. Engineers and inventors are needed to plan the production of rails and locomotives, to learn and teach the art of bridge-making, to discover the possibilities of telegraphy, and invent a system of signalling. What genuine admiration beavers ought to feel for our great bridges and tunnels!

Another army of workers must fashion a permanent way, build embankments, manufacture rails, make stations, signal-boxes, and rolling stock. And while the navvies are raising an embankment and steelmakers are making rails, they must be fed, clothed, and housed; for the first income from a railway is obtained long after the beginning of the work which is being done by the labourers. Someone else, then, who is actually in possession of an income, must save part of it, and must be willing to allow the workers to use it.

But we have forgotten *The Admirable Crichton* and our desert island. Let us return to the marooned Lord Loam, his nephew Ernest, and his daughter the Lady Mary. The following extract will help us:

ERNEST (with greedy cunning). "You are actually wearing boots, Uncle. It's very unsafe, you know, in this climate."

LADY MARY (quickly). "Father, he is trying to get your boots from you. There is nothing in the world we wouldn't give for boots."

The possession of boots seems ordinarily quite unworthy of special attention; but, after all, how could Ernest, marooned on the island, obtain a pair? How do we obtain them in England?

The first part of the answer to this question is concerned with cattle—and it may be that they are roaming in some far-away country like South America. Leaving the cowboys and their prairies our cattle reach the ocean, make use of a steamship, and, aided by men who understand navigation, they disembark at some foreign animals' wharf in our country. It now becomes a question of hides rather than of animals. The hide factor now appears and is observed to be selling his wares to a tanner. In places like Bermondsey, the hides are tanned and dressed, after which we have to do with finished leather. Other agents, factories, and machines are needed now, for in towns like Northampton, the leather suffers another change, and appears finally in the form of boots and shoes.

If all this seems very simple, the story of the laces

might now be told, their adventures in the warehouses of the wholesale dealers, and the final act of distribution in the retail shop.

A very interesting question arises at this stage. Would some of our present wants disappear on a desert island?

Readers of *The Admirable Crichton* will remember that at length the rescue ship appeared, and the last act of the play took place in London. It was then that Lord Loam confessed that his needs had undergone a change. Consider collars, for example. "As for my clothes," he said, wriggling, "you can't think how irksome collars are to me nowadays."

However did the taste for collars—and especially starched ones—develop? It would surely come rather late in the story of a complete outfit. The habits of many men with regard to collars seemed to be changing during the Great War. It was quite common to hear recruits say, "Well, at any rate, I have done with collars for ever." If those recruits are now alive, they are probably wearing collars to-day. So difficult to understand are the wants of man!

A marooned sailor has no chance whatever of obtaining a new collar. How do we get them ourselves?

The peasant reaping flax in a country like Russia plays a large part in the story. His labour, however, could have little to do with the manufacture of collars had not some captain of industry devised a method by which Russian flax can be conveyed to Belfast and used there. The thinker who can plan and carry out an operation like this is much more difficult to discover and train than an ordinary peasant. From Russian flax, then, Irish linen can be manufactured. Then machinery from countries like the United States and Scotland may be used in Leicester to produce collars. Nor could the work be carried on without iron, steel, coal, railways, shipping, and the use of money. The money paid for a collar by a smart young fellow in a London shop may enable a Russian peasant to buy a cup of tea from China, or a cigarette from Cuba.

Peasants, then, must plant and reap flax, stokers must shovel coal into a steamship to bring the flax to Belfast, miners must hew the coal that is necessary, railwaymen must handle the linen. It is necessary for factories to be built and for machines to be planned and made. In the factories at Leicester and Belfast, men and women, boys and girls, are employed in turning handles and moving levers. Merchants then purchase collars, and polite salesmen sell them.

But more must be considered than labour. What of the land that grew the flax? Could a collar be manufactured without lubricating oil? No steamer could transport flax without this oil; all the machinery at Belfast and Leicester needs it; it is necessary for every railway train and delivery van. Many things are necessary before a collar can be produced. Labour is one essential factor, land and lubricating oil are included among the others.

In the modern store we see around us the products of many lands. The finished goods placed before our gaze in the shop windows and on the counters seem to differ from one another in every sort of way; but they are alike in this one respect at least: they all cost something; they are all forms which wealth may take.

In studying further the many processes which lead to the production of wealth, it will be a great help to remember as much as possible of the objects by which we are thus surrounded in our everyday life. All that relates to our food, all that we can learn about our clothing will furnish a good beginning; then we may advance to try to trace the many processes which precede the appearance on the counter of other goods to supply other wants.

It has already been noted, for example, that the rubber planter is one of the pillars of a modern city. To him we owe the motor-car tyre, the rubber toy, and the rubber mat. Rubber is even used for paving some streets.

Again we find a team of workers. The rubber planter owes much to chemistry. It was the chemist who found a method by which rubber could be made so hard and solid that even in hot weather it ceased to be sticky. The result was brought about by the addition of sulphur, and the application of much heat. Then rubber, which obtained its name through its modest job of rubbing out pencil marks, was used to make a cloth through which water would not pass— the mackintosh. When a great amount of sulphur is added to rubber, vulcanite or ebonite is produced; and then fountain pens appear on the counter.

Columbus, who first saw the West Indian children playing with bouncing balls of rubber, was without doubt a great adventurer; but the story of rubber did not become a romance of commerce until long after the death of the prince of explorers. When the wild rubber trees were becoming very scarce in South

America, 7000 rubber seeds were hurried from the River Amazon to the glass-houses in Kew Gardens by a worthy knight of commerce in the year 1876. Soon little rubber trees were seen in outer London. Many of them were sent to Ceylon and Malaya. Thus appeared the rubber plantations which produce the rubber juice of modern trade.

The story of a pair of silk stockings is as interesting as that of a rubber ball. A fellow-worker in this industry is the lazy easy-going moth which we call a silkworm. Its chief work, beyond a little aimless flying hither and thither, is to lay a large number of eggs before it dies. From these eggs the little silkworms are hatched. These must be fed with the leaves of the mulberry tree. The silkworm when fully grown produces a silky material. Its life-work is to spin the cocoon. Women and children in China and Japan look after the silkworms. They used to reel off the silk by hand, but now most of that work is done in factories. After reeling, the hanks of raw silk known to our industry appear. The story of the manufacture of silk machines in France and England is as wonderful as that of the working caterpillar. Machines twist the raw silk into thread, then weave it into cloth, or knit it into stockings.

Recent inventors have found ways of producing a silky material which resembles the natural silk. The silkworms make their silk by forcing a sort of jelly through two tiny holes in their heads. When this jelly-like substance hardens in the air, it forms raw silk. To make artificial silk the chemist helps, as he did in the case of soft rubber. He adds some chemicals to wood pulp and short waste hairs of cotton to make his jelly. The jelly is then forced through very small tubes, it is passed through a drying bath, and may then be spun and woven. Thus do silkworms, mulberry leaves, women, children, men, machines and different countries, all co-operate in process after process before a finished product is offered for sale in a shop!

QUESTIONS AND EXERCISES

1. Select some article in common use, and explain very generally the processes by which it is produced.

2. Explain the needs of any native population, *e.g.* the West African negroes, and show to what extent they are supplied by means of commerce.

3. What goods would probably be offered for sale by the only shopkeeper in a small English village?

4. What do you mean by necessaries and luxuries? Mention different types of people of both sexes, to make the meaning of your answer clearer.

5. Describe the various ways in which a provision merchant in a large town may deliver his goods. Assume that he has some country customers.

CHAPTER IV

WORK, SKILL, AND PROGRESS

Our subject now is the way in which human services have been rendered from time to time: it is, in short, the rough story of work.

The needs of primitive man led to the invention of weapons and tools. When cries, calls, growls, and grunts had had their day, the spirit of man demanded the invention of human speech. This growing activity of mind and body led to the increasing use of great natural forces. Thus man desired and obtained better food, clothing, and the comforts of a rude home.

In very early times it became clear that certain kinds of work were regarded as being more suitable for women than men. Thus men made weapons and hunted animals, while women tended the children and cooked food.

Certain gifted individuals would then show special skill in mending and making tools, while others might reveal exceptional cleverness in preparing skins for clothing. Picture then each member of a group engaged upon work which suits him. The hunter must then exchange part of the spoils of the chase for weapons and clothes. As man continued to make use of his experience and progressed, there would be many more distinct and separate callings. The craftsman is no longer the same person as the priest or medical man, for the latter is believed to be specially skilful in dealing with evil spirits. The potter is unable to make dwellings, the breeders of flocks and herds, and the growers of corn, are unable to make a sickle. One man may make a stone hand-mill, another may fashion skin bottles, a third may be a baker. So man relies more and more on the help of his fellows for what he is unable to produce himself, and a simple form of trade becomes more and more necessary. Man for the most part no longer consumes his own products, but the goods of others which he secures through barter. Thus corn is exchanged for meat, an axe may be bartered for clothes, or a rude dwelling may be exchanged for a number of animals.

Distinct callings for different men were found convenient, in spite of the disadvantages of the system of barter. The leather workers were not skilled in weaving, the man who could make a plough did not actually use it himself to produce corn, the shepherd was a different person from the miner. But all these men in their different ways did something for their fellows.

It will be useful, in connection with this question of the division of labour, if we think once more of the Loam House party mentioned in *The Admirable Crichton*. Before arriving at their desert island in the Pacific, they have been used to the life of Mayfair. At Loam House, London, there is much labour, and it is minutely divided. The admirable Crichton is the perfect butler; he does not act as a clergyman, for example, for a young minister is mentioned in the story. The division of labour among the servants is very interesting. There is, as a matter of fact, what may be termed a subdivision of labour, as may be seen from the following dialogue:

LADY MARY. "What is your position downstairs?"

TWEENY (bobbing). "I'm a tweeny, your ladyship."

CATHERINE. "A what?"

CRICHTON. "A tweeny; that is, to say, my lady, she is not at present, strictly speaking, anything; a *between* maid; she helps the vegetable maid. It is she, my lady, who conveys the dishes from one end of the kitchen table, where they are placed by the cook, to the other end, where they enter into the charge of Thomas and John."

Here is division of labour indeed! We are now better able to trace the work of the builders of cities. The earliest settlements of which we read are very easy to understand. Even an intelligent rabbit, in fact, might have grasped the plan of the burrows of the cave-dwellers. It was when small clusters of huts appeared on the surface of the earth that the earliest problems in planning settlements were solved. It was not necessary to take into account more than the big simple things of human life. The hut-dwellers had enemies. The settlements, then, appeared at the edges of rivers, lakes, and marshes. From a lake fish could be obtained, while a clearing in the forest would provide ground for cultivation. Caddles the giant could have understood all this. The problems suggested by his own chalk-pit were as difficult as those of the hut-dwellers in their villages.

But the tribe grows. Hill forts are planned. Life is becoming more complicated. A simple form of trade develops. Every sphere of life shows change: iron implements displace those of bronze; cemeteries take the place of barrows; there are roads and vehicles, and, at length, towns.

Some landmarks may easily be observed in the history of our own country. All that relates to an early English village, for example, is very interesting, and can be understood without much difficulty. The settlement at this stage consisted chiefly of the homes of farmers, so its site would be selected from the point of view of farming alone. Of course a water supply would be necessary. Very often we find that these ancient villages were built on high land about half a mile from a road or river. This enabled the villagers to avoid unpleasant wayfarers, and to live in the midst of their cultivated lands. Apart from trade in such articles as salt, such a village would be what we call self-contained : practically all the simple needs of the people would be supplied within the settlement itself. The local river would drive the mill; from the surrounding woods timber and fuel would be obtained; rabbits and other game would be available; and neighbouring pits might provide marl for the lands on which the life of the village depended. The homes of the villagers would be found on either side of a little street, the lord's residence being usually built in the highest part of the village. When the lord's dwelling became the manor house, a church would be built near it.

But, as we know, the villages did not remain self-contained for ever, and the high roads of the country were soon associated with merchants rather than robbers. As trade increased, the villagers migrated to the highways to share in the profits which were to be obtained by means of the traffic on the roads. It was easier, however, to remove the peasants' huts than the church and the manor. Does not this explain why we sometimes find a church and an old manor house standing apart from the main village which stretches along a high road?

If the manorial village prospers, the market town is bound to come next. Think of some of the things that would have to be provided, in addition to clothing and food. There would be casks and cups, of course, with boilers, benches, stools and tables. But what about bill-hooks, spades, and the hedger's gloves? The carpenter would have no difficulty in obtaining well-seasoned wood in the required quantities, but how would the smith obtain iron? Not in every manorial village would crude lumps of this necessary metal be available. Only by means of trade, as a rule, could the villages obtain the iron tools of which they knew full well the value. The smith, as a matter of fact, in the later period of the manorial system, had to travel to some neighbouring fair in a market town to purchase his raw materials. How did these towns develop?

The lure of the highways, as we have already said, was the steadily increasing traffic. Then at the intersection of roads, or near a ford or a bridge, or to supply a population brought together by a monastery or a castle, a town would grow. In these settlements the people depended for their livelihood mainly upon their market. A common plan is often found for these towns. One of the roads in the centre of the settlement was generally widened at one end, and this space became the market-place. Then the lord of the soil would attract settlers by granting them timber and materials for the building of houses. The boundary of a market-place was often for a time dotted with very frail booths and stalls; but each tenant to whom a plot of land was allotted would undertake to build, within a measurable time, a house or shop-front in the market-place. There the frontage of the settler's plot would be narrow, but it usually stretched away to the rear as far as the town boundary, and included later, gardens and orchards. All the roads of the settlement, then, met in the market-place, and thus all the traffic of the highways was compelled to pass through the town. The commerce of the roads was also made to pay its toll at many an old-world ford, bridge, or ferry.

Attention has often been drawn to the ancient city of Salisbury in connection with town-planning. We are not at all surprised when we read that Bishop Poore in the thirteenth century had the famous cathedral of this old city built according to plan; but it is somewhat astonishing to learn that the old bishop planned the town itself in considerable detail: in very truth he "pegged out a whole brand-new city on a houseless field."

Old Salisbury or Sarum certainly existed before the thirteenth century. It was a typical hill-town of the period, containing castle, cathedral, and the homes of the citizens.

But there was every sort of discomfort in the city which had grown, as people say, naturally: there was hardly room for the citizens to move within the narrow compass of the flat summit; there was no protection from the storms; the water supply was bad;

and much labour was wasted in transporting goods to the markets and fairs on the hill.

Two miles to the south the bishop owned a rich area of meadow land through which the Avon flows. In the thirteenth century when the protection of the castle on the hill was becoming less necessary, many citizens began to migrate to the plain. In 1220, in fact, Bishop Poore began to transfer his cathedral there.

But he did more than this. With other local lords he planned a city suitable for craftsmen. He arranged to let out his land in plots, which were grouped in parallelograms.

The plan on page 42, taken from Speed's *Theatre of Great Britain*, 1676, London, shows how it was made possible for the new town to possess streets wide enough for the traffic of a market town.

In some cases small streams useful for drainage were included in the plan. This seemed, no doubt, very advanced in the thirteenth century: sanitation was then thought to be excellent if there was access to a water supply, with gutters to carry away the rain-water. Each householder was allowed sufficient land for a garden, but not enough for farming. Plenty of space was left for markets where the roads to Old Sarum and Wilton crossed each other. This was important to a city of craftsmen: it was also important to the Old Seignior, for his income depended upon his market dues. The new city was more central than the old one; thus, apart from the absence of the hill of Old Sarum, the transport of goods was easier. The Avon had to be crossed by traffic from the west, but this was provided for by a new bridge across the river.

This changed Salisbury, then, was our first garden city. Its trade also flourished in the new circumstances. Wool, for example, was easily collected from the valleys around, water for washing it was abundant, and there was no obstacle to its distribution to London,

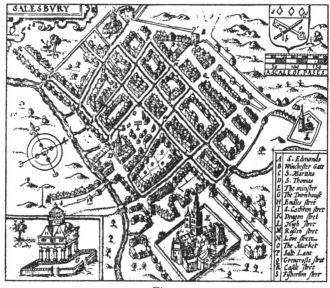

Fig. 4

Bristol, and Southampton. Hence the growing wool trade, and later the cloth industry, continued to attract new settlers to take up plots of land. Not only did they come from the overcrowded upland of Old Sarum, but also from Wilton three miles to the west; and the trade of that once prosperous borough passed to the new Salisbury. In vain did the men of Wilton,

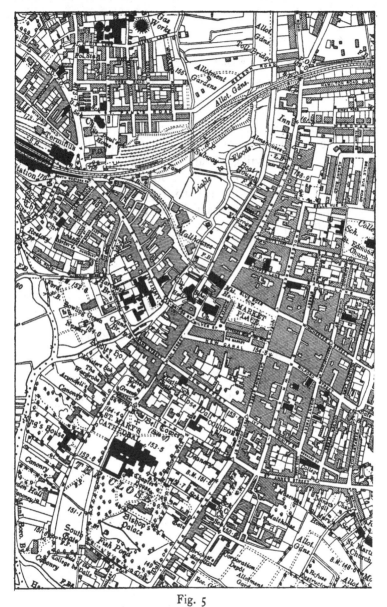

Fig. 5

Reproduced from the Ordnance Survey Map with the sanction of the Controller of
H.M. Stationery Office

angry at the loss of their customers, try to force the traders of the district to bring their goods as before to the old market. The prosperity of the new Salisbury was assured.

Thus were laid the foundations of one of our modern cities. It is easier to understand the simple society of the manorial village than the Salisbury of the middle ages. But the township of long ago has become a much more difficult maze to-day. The Ordnance Survey map of modern Salisbury reveals many relics of the town plan of the thirteenth century, but also many developments of which the old bishop never dreamt.

QUESTIONS AND EXERCISES

1. Write an account of village life in England either

   (a) at the present time, or

   (b) at any period before 1200.

2. Can you imagine a market in early times with exchanges of goods taking place by barter, *i.e.* without the help of money?

3. What inventions can you think of that give help to the housewife in her work?

4. How many different groups of workmen co-operate in the building of a small dwelling house?

5. What do you mean by Division of Labour in industry? Try to show how it began.

6. Show what assistance is given by tools to any workman whom you know.

7. Write down as full a list as you can of all the jobs that must be carried out by different workers before band music can be broadcast.

8. Give as many examples as you can of:

(*a*) the human porter,

(*b*) pack animals,

(*c*) animals used for drawing vehicles along roads.

Show how mechanical transport is more and more replacing these services.

CHAPTER V

THE HELPERS OF THE WORKERS

A famous American will now tell us of the helpers of the work of man. "For," he writes, "the weary camels in the desert caravan, the huge draught horses in the great vehicles of transport in our cities, the ploughing bullock, and the racing hound, all help to supply human wants. Sometimes the creatures of nature alone without the help of man suffice to produce wealth in certain forms. Consider, for example, the natural increase of a herd of cattle; think of the little silkworm; remember the lore of the honey-bee. But as a rule man obtains the best help possible by harnessing the powers of nature and directing them. In this way the power of the winds was used in very early days for mill and sail, to grind corn and to pump water. Sometimes one force of nature has been used to defeat another: thus the steam-driven vessel is independent of the gales and is able to defy them. Man now makes use of air and sea and land for transport. It is in the air that the flying machine travels, and by means of dirigible airships carrying heavy loads man may make use of the atmosphere in the distribution of goods. The use to be made of the oceans we appreciate more easily; for the surface steamer and the underwater craft must both receive attention. Without fresh water human life would disappear, and almost all wares at some time or other are afloat on the ocean highways. The running stream has turned the water-wheel for past generations; what will the tides do in the future?"

Let us think next of fuel, especially coal and oil. It is by means of huge furnaces that mighty work is done with metals; it is through steam that factories, railways, and ocean transport have changed the conditions of life. The new use of the high roads by oil-driven vehicles has been one of the most striking changes of our own time; for the petrol engine is a modern invention which has revealed new and vast possibilities in transport and industry.

Nor should magnetism and electricity be forgotten. We know how epoch-making in economic history was the discovery of the uses of the mariner's compass. The electric vehicle of to-day reveals in a flash how mysterious and mighty are the natural forces that in our time have been harnessed in the service of mankind. We remember the telephone and the cable; we have witnessed the revelation of radio. In inquiring into the business of man in the ordinary relations of life, the help given by nature was for a curiously long time represented by land alone; and it seemed much to understand the benefit to crops of the chemical reactions that take place in the earth and to know something of the effects of heat and moisture on plant life. Then the story of the domestication of animals seemed to mark another great landmark in the history of human effort when applied to the production of wealth. But the mightiest changes have been effected by the harnessing of the great forces of nature as revealed by science in the service of human workers; and the progress continues from day to day.

In the older books we notice that the term "land" is used as a sort of shorthand, including in its meaning such things as coal seams, minerals, mineral springs, and rivers, as well as farms. The use of land to labour is very much like the uses of the raw materials, the tools with which man works, and the food, clothing, and shelter which must be provided while the work is progressing. The word "capital" is really the best to describe all these aids of labour. Among these allies we have already spoken of bill-hooks, ploughs, mills, roads, bridges, vehicles of various kinds, houses, clothes, farm-buildings, casks, spades, benches, and hedgers' gloves in manorial villages. In towns like the new Salisbury we can well understand that the carpenters, smiths, and especially the craftsmen of the wool industry would need more and more helpers of the same kind in the form of equipment for their work. Even Caddles in his chalk-pit made use of pick-axe, spade, and the rolling stock of a light railway; so he should have been quite ready to understand a lesson on capital.

One of the outstanding differences between the old-fashioned towns and those of modern times is due to this very whirring of wheels. Since the eighteenth century the forms of wealth which wear away in the act of producing more wealth have been increasing at a very rapid rate.

A great Austrian economist has pointed out that the human hand is too rude for the finest work, so a microscope must be used; on the other hand it is too feeble for other jobs, e.g. smashing rocks, so blasting powder must be employed. The same teacher quotes the case of a man who lived near a river, and at first had to go to the water himself whenever he felt thirsty. At length he made himself a wooden bucket and brought home a whole day's supply at a time. This wooden bucket was a form of what is called capital : its job was to aid human labour. A huge stock of goods is available in our cities for this purpose.

By means of more capital our water-drinker saved himself even the daily journey to the river with his wooden bucket. He took some hollowed logs, arranged them end to end from the bank to his home, and made a conduit which brought him a regular supply of water.

In our cities more capital still is used to ensure a satisfactory water supply. Coal and iron mines, brick kilns, and steel works are used for this same purpose. How is this? Think of the pumping machinery, the plant for purifying the water, the cisterns and pipes and taps in every house! Think of the bricks and mortar, the steel and the concrete which is necessary to capture the wild and whirling river in its mountain home! All the forms of capital which we have mentioned are needed to help to fill the reservoirs. We find when we trace the manufacture of goods that capital helps labour to produce nearly all the stocks in our shops. The story begins with the work of man in the fields or waste places, but it ends with the labour of citizens in their works and factories amid the din of machinery. We may commence with the simple and soothing old-world occupations of silk-worms and peasants, but we shall yet end our tale with a record of the whirring of some of the most wonderful machines in the Great Industry. Even the story of a cup of tea cannot be told without accompanying references to railway, steamship, and warehouse.

Flowers and potatoes satisfy human wants directly —at once. The men who planned and carried out the manufacture of spades really wanted potatoes and flowers to appear in the long run, but they aimed at getting them by what is sometimes called the round-about process, the use of capital. They sought their ends indirectly, they brought in allies, and found the roundabout way to be the better of the two. When men really desire to obtain potatoes but first manufacture spades as a help, the process is not direct: that is why we say that the use of capital is the round-about method of production. But by means of capital, *e.g.* with the help of spades, potatoes and flowers can in the long run be obtained much more easily and in greater quantities.

Of course a spade is a form of wealth. It has a money value. But it can be used only to help to produce fresh wealth: that is why we call it a form of capital. Some skilled workers owe much to capital.

One is inclined to say at once that there is nothing roundabout in connection with a busy doctor, for example, since he is able to reach a sick person with the greatest rapidity. He certainly does not seem to have any preference for roundabout routes.

It is true that the human service rendered by a doctor is prompt enough; but is there nothing at all roundabout in the methods by which his efficiency has been rendered possible? Our doctor was once a boy, and in that far-away time, food, clothing and shelter were provided for him when he was not able to render many services in return for what he received. Schools, teachers and books were all necessary. Scholars in colleges, the knowledge to be obtained in the great hospitals, now come into the story, with scientific instruments and medicines.

After a long period of preparation our doctor was thus able to commence his blessed work of healing; but even now he has to lean heavily upon those who produce cars, books, instruments and drugs from every clime to render his services more efficient.

A sick person, then, when receiving medical treatment receives the benefit of much capital. From the point of view of the preparation for the necessary duties of a healer, there is no short cut to the sick-room. A doctor must make unceasing use of a library of scientific knowledge and almost a warehouse of scientific equipment. His road to his patient leads through school, college and hospital; it is quite as roundabout as the other routes which we have noted.

A bootmaker may himself purchase leather, and by means of a few simple tools he may make a pair of boots. But the tools had to be made for him: they are a form of capital, for they are used to produce wealth.

As a rule, however, capital is of far greater service in manufacturing boots than in the case of the cobbler working alone. Huge quantities of raw materials are purchased, mills are necessary, machinery must be employed, warehouses are built, and shops of retailers are used.

When a machine replaces a workman we may say that capital replaces labour. It is clear that a machine works more rapidly than a man. Of course it takes time to make the machinery, and to build the mills, warehouses, and shops; but think of the vast masses of boots which are now manufactured. In former days a cobbler would make a pair of shoes and then begin another. If at the present time a particular boot is traced from the beginning of the processes in a factory to the end, the course seems long and roundabout: *i.e.* it seems to take a long time to make each boot.

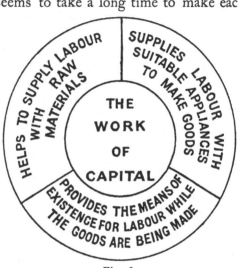

Fig. 6

But great quantities of boots are being made at the same time. At any given instant the raw material is entering the factory at one end, and many boots are being finished at the other.

It is not always easy to tell whether a particular thing is capital or not. The thing itself may not change, but its use may. Here is a piece of wood, a board! It is lying in a workman's shed, and it will remain a board, of course, until we can trace it no further. But is it a form of capital? That is a question which will be decided by the use to which the board is put. If our workman uses it to help to make the floor of a factory, the board becomes a form of capital. But who can foretell its future? It may be consumed in adding brightness to the festivities at the local inn. It will not then be worn away or consumed in the making of fresh wealth.

Another rather startling idea relating to capital may be introduced by a somewhat soothing quotation from a writer of the twelfth century:

"Among the noble cities of the world that fame celebrates, the city of London is the one that pours out its fame more widely, sends to fresh lands its trade and wealth, and lifts its head higher than the rest.... On the north side there are pastures and pleasant meadowland, through which flow river streams, where the turning wheels of mills are put in motion with a cheerful sound."

No doubt in those rather easier times a new water-wheel was never made until the old one was worn out. But the modern type of water-wheel, called a water turbine, is much more cleverly devised than the old-fashioned wheel with its wooden paddles. In our days, even if certain forms of capital are not consumed—even if they are not actually worn away in the service of man—they must sometimes be scrapped, as we say, when better machines to do the particular work are invented. With forms of capital which are out-of-date, labour is severely handicapped.

The study of mankind, then, in the ordinary business of civic life is really the study of the output, transport, and distribution of goods and services. Money is merely anything in the shape of coins or paper instruments that is commonly taken in exchange for these goods and services. Near the byways are to be found or cultivated the necessary materials which

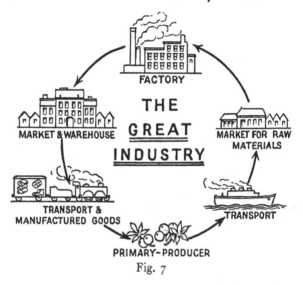

FACTORY

THE GREAT INDUSTRY

MARKET & WAREHOUSE

MARKET FOR RAW MATERIALS

TRANSPORT & MANUFACTURED GOODS

TRANSPORT

PRIMARY-PRODUCER

Fig. 7

have to be obtained from kindly Mother Earth by her children. These raw materials are transported to the highways of industry; and there the freights are delivered at great factories and manufactured into finished goods by means of labour and great machines. Then the finished goods pass by means of other busy workers, and great vans, oil-driven cars, railways, ocean vessels and airships to the markets of the world.

We have now, it may be, been able to understand to some extent how the throngs of men in a modern city gain through a union of forces. In the game of business life the investor and the inventor, the wage-earner and the employer all have their allotted positions, and if one fails the whole team suffers loss.

The sports ground is unusual: it is not compact like the school playing-fields: the street and the market-place are part of it, the farm and the stock exchange must be added, and the pavilion is formed by the factory and the bank. Victory is won when wealth is produced in abundance and shared fairly; and the team as a whole receives credit for the result. The goal which gives special delight to the captain of the lucky side is due primarily, it may be, to another player; for the goods which give us the greatest enjoyment of all may be due to the labour of other men.

QUESTIONS AND EXERCISES

1. A market gardener receives a legacy of £300, buys an extra plot of land, and on it grows potatoes for sale. What forms of capital will assist his labour?

2. Does a boy or girl obtain any help from capital while at school?

3. What occupation would you like to follow in later life? What assistance would be given by capital to you and your fellow-workers?

4. Show in what ways a farmer at the present time is helped by capital.

5. Explain how important it is for people to be thrifty.

6. Give some examples to show how much industry owes to the inventors of new machines, geographical discoverers, and great engineers.

7. A lady living in the Manchester district wishes to purchase flowering shrubs and rose trees from Dunfermline, but does not wish to go there. Show how she can buy from Scotland by making use of the newspaper, the Post Office, the catalogue of the Dunfermline firm, and the railway.

CHAPTER VI

MONEY IS AS MONEY DOES

Our more lively newspapers would, in these days, be delighted to discover someone who was trying to supply all his wants without the help of, and without giving help to, his fellows. The ordinary worker, of course, now helps to make one thing only, or to render to others only one kind of service. He himself, in return, asks for many: it is not very different to say that he asks for money. For the chief use of money is to render the exchange of commodities and services easier.

All sorts of goods at different times have been employed as money. The Mexicans have used cocoa to pay for things. Drinking cocoa was then really drinking money. Here is a surprising sentence from an old writer: "Cocoa passed current as money among all peoples in Central America at this time: thus a rabbit in Nicaragua sold for ten cocoa nibs, and one hundred of these seeds would buy a tolerably good slave." This seems very strange indeed to one who at once thinks of gold, silver or copper when money is mentioned. Even in our own country the actual medium of exchange has altered very much recently: the use of paper as money has become far commoner in our time than formerly.

It is not always easy to say exactly what is meant by the term "money," for money is as money does. At any rate it is clear that it is something which has had to be invented in order to help producers of goods to

exchange them; and we have also noticed that all
sorts of things have been thus used. If any particular
article was fairly common, and was desired by many
producers of goods, it was usually fairly easy to use
it in the exchange of commodities. We have read the
record of cocoa having been thus employed in trade,
but nuts, dates, salt, and even dried fish have served
as money. At one time it was most important for each
man to possess weapons; hence knives and sword-hilts
formed the money of that period. If we know when
shovels and hoes were used as money by a particular
tribe, we have a good idea as to the economic progress
of the people concerned. No longer do they roam
from place to place—the nomadic stage has passed.
No longer is hunting their only occupation. A settlement has been made, and agriculture is important to
them. We may well expect that flocks and herds will
appear in our list of moneys at some time or other;
and, as a matter of fact, sheep and oxen have served
as media of exchange for many peoples. When the
eye of the scholar is riveted on the word "pecuniary,"
there is visible to him—although far away—the oxen
of which we are now speaking. When man became
civilized enough to value his clothing very highly, and
when the increasing cold led to his need for warm
coverings, leather, skins, and furs were used to purchase other goods and to pay debts, *i.e.* these commodities were used as money.

But as wealth increased and ornaments were more
highly valued, feathers, shells and beads served to
measure the value of other things, and to assist trade.
With the discovery of the uses of metals, copper,

bronze, tin and iron were used as money. At the present time a bar of gold is very welcome in a bank; but for quite a long time iron was used by merchants as a medium of exchange and a measure of value. Silver and gold were for ages the most useful forms of the money of civilized peoples.

It is possible to imagine a household in early times which supplied all its simple wants by means of its own labour. It built a primitive house, made rough clothes, tended and used certain domestic animals, tilled the earth and reaped its own crops. But at length it would be found that the land of one household produced better wheat more readily than that of another, while oil might be directly exchanged for wheat, wine, cotton, sugar in some form, or tobacco. This is an example of what we have called direct barter, and it has been seen how awkward the system was. Imagine a man with a surplus of wheat who desired to barter some of it for tobacco. He might find a trader with a surplus of tobacco, but how disappointed he would be if this particular merchant had enough wheat and wished to barter his tobacco for wine. It is thus easy to understand why it was found necessary to select one particular commodity which everyone would be glad to accept, and to use it as money. Thus when rice was so used it was because everyone knew that he could obtain any other goods by means of his rice. Now imagine a trader with a surplus of tea who desires to purchase salt. He may possibly know another merchant with a surplus of salt who does not desire tea. However, both know the value of rice, and are aware that it is generally desired by the people, some of whom have stores of it. It is now possible for the tea to be exchanged for rice, and then for the rice to be offered for salt. Rice is thus the medium by means of which tea is exchanged for salt. The amount of rice employed in the transaction has been used to measure the values of the tea and the salt.

We can understand, then, why the traders accept rice in exchange for their wares. But what would have been the astonishment of the merchants of that time if someone had offered them, not rice, but a piece of paper on which was written or printed the statement that it was worth a certain quantity of rice. We shall have to speak of the Government and banks of our country in a later chapter, but we will, for the time being, merely draw attention to the printed notes which they issue, and which we use as money. We credit the statements made on them. "The Bank of England promises to pay the bearer on demand the sum of One Pound." That is practically all that is printed on one particular note. Thus banknotes are not really a means of final payment. They are merely promises to pay. Until recently these notes could be exchanged for gold to the amount named. This system is referred to as that of the Gold Standard.

Such an arrangement is specially convenient for the purposes of foreign trade, for gold has an international value. But at present, in 1932, the Bank of England is not obliged to pay the bearer of a pound note that value in gold coin. The value of British paper money depends now more than ever upon the credit of the Government, which works hand in hand with the Bank of England. These notes are the chief means by which we exchange goods and services. The right amount of money has to be put into circulation to do its proper work. Paper money is useless in commerce if traders do not believe that it can be exchanged for desirable goods.

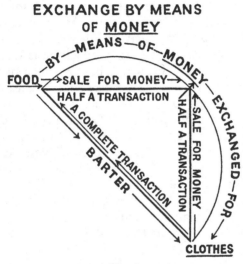

Fig. 8

We are now better able to trace the stages of progress in connection with the production and exchange of goods. In the first place we have seen the primitive household with no great need of commodities which it does not itself produce. Then comes the system of direct barter through the exchange, for example, of oil for wheat. But the awkwardness of this arrangement leads to the invention of a better system, although it seems more roundabout. With the use of money we have what may be called triangular barter: oil, for example, may now be exchanged for rice, and rice in turn offered for wheat. In this way oil is really exchanged for wheat. Then finally credit money is introduced. This is the stage at which we have at present arrived.

This arrangement permits a man to work for others, and enables others to work for him. Here is a chauffeur who knows quite well that he will need food, clothes, and amusements, for example, which he is unable to provide for himself. He would be very much surprised if at the end of a week he was paid by means of a paper containing upon its surface a statement something like the following: "Other people in your working group are hereby instructed to make for you a new pair of boots, to reap corn for you, to make you bread and cakes, to kill animals and supply you with meat, to grow cotton for you in America and transport it to England, to manufacture cloth and to make you a cotton garment."

Yet in practice something like this happens. Our worker when his job is done is usually given a piece of paper on which are printed certain statements. These statements are believed by other workers to be true. Hence they are willing to accept certain definite orders from the driver of the car. He knows what his mates are doing, and can see in the retail shops the goods they have produced. In return for his paper, or part of it, they are willing to supply him with the goods which he desires. Of course, the function of his paper as a measure of value, as well as its work as a medium of exchange, must be borne in mind. He sees, then, around him millions of workers engaged in the Great

Industry, and his paper money enables him to decide which groups shall render him service. It even enables him to decide, to some extent, what work shall be performed by others and what jobs shall cease.

It seems on examination a very fair arrangement. Here is an individual associated with crowds of other workers. "We desire you," they say in effect, "to take orders from us up to a point, and we will then, more or less, obey you. If you are a miner, it is your job to hew coal for us. If you serve us in that way we will serve you in others. In return for your work for us you shall command our services, you shall give us orders."

This is a sort of social and economic bargain. In accordance with its terms a man through his skill and labour obtains the right to decide how others shall work in return to pay him for his efforts. After successful toil on his own part a sort of tribute is levied on others by the worker. The value to others of the labour of a worker is measured by means of the wages paid to him in money. Then we may say that the value of our miner's work to the world is equal to the cost of the pleasures and comforts which he obtains in return.

It is when he spends his money that a labourer issues commands: he then ceases to be what is sometimes wrongly called a wage-slave, and becomes just as much, in his new capacity as a spender, a wage-emperor. Our workers, of course, are neither slaves nor emperors: they simply receive orders with regard to their own work and, to some extent, issue them with regard to the services of others. When a workman refuses to buy clogs and spends his money on leather boots, he is practically ordering certain workers to make no more clogs. If a miner buys a gas mantle he is in practice saying to his fellow-workers, "From now make very few oil lamps, but manufacture gas fittings instead." He may in our own time say, when spending his wages, "I now ask a group of workers to manufacture electrical fittings."

Of course paper would not be accepted in payment for services unless it was believed that it could be exchanged for goods. The element of belief shows that we are here dealing with credit money.

A well-known writer on money quotes a world-famous old Spanish story. He shows Don Quixote releasing from the grip of the law a rascal who at once proceeded to steal his servant Sancho Panza's ass. But Don Quixote had many asses wandering in the Sierra Morena, and he consoled Sancho Panza with a piece of paper money, which was to be exchanged for what was required by the victim of the donkey thief. The paper he received from the Don was really a sort of credit instrument, and Sancho Panza valued it because of his belief that it could be exchanged for donkeys. The asses were more or less in the charge of the Don's niece, and the statement on what we may call the piece of paper money was as follows:

"Dear Niece, At sight of this, my first bill of ass-colts, give order that three out of the five I left at home in your custody be delivered to Sancho Panza, my squire; which three colts I order to be delivered and paid for the like number received of him here in tale; and this, with his acquittance, shall be your discharge."

"Done in the heart of the Sierra Morena, the 22nd of August, this present year."

"It is mighty well," said Sancho, "Now you have only to sign it."

"It wants no signing," said Don Quixote, "I need only put my cipher to it, which is the same thing, and is sufficient, not only for three, but for three hundred asses."

The credit money issued by Don Quixote was as useful as a bar of gold on the donkey market.

Two very different uses of money must always be kept in mind. There is money which we pay away in the form of coins or notes to satisfy our everyday wants. But there is also money which is saved. The latter is not now hoarded in a stocking or a drawer: it is lent—it is loaned for the service of us all. Of course this money must be returned at a later date to the lender, and what is called Interest must be paid for the use of it. Ready money is exchanged by the lender for the promise (which he credits) of more money some day. The amount paid as Interest must be sufficient to induce people to save and to lend. Some such inducement as the following may be supposed to be addressed to a man with money to spend :

"To pay you for your labour by which services have been rendered to others, you have received buying power worth, let us say, a suit of clothes of fair quality. But at present you are not in actual want of clothes, nor of anything else of the kind; hence you can well postpone the purchase without loss of actual comfort.

We have just now need in agriculture of more spades. If you are willing to allow your buying power to be used to help us to obtain spades, food and employment will be more abundant for others. In addition to this, remember that after a time you will receive back enough money to enable you to purchase a suit of better quality of cloth than you could at present obtain."

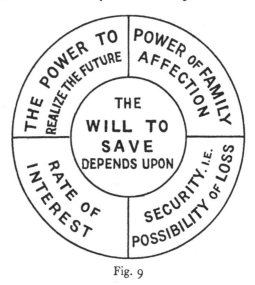

Fig. 9

. The work done by money is so important that we shall do well to collect all our ideas on the subject before we make another advance.

We understand, then, that paper or credit money has no value apart from the things which it enables people to buy. Without money and credit our system of exchange could not work at all; thus division of labour, which requires a system of exchange of goods, depends on money. A great teacher has compared money to a cloak-room ticket: it is the coat that gives the warmth, but it is the ticket that can be exchanged for the coat.

Many details of our monetary system we all know from our ordinary use of money and our arithmetical calculations. It is easy to understand why so many coins are necessary. If we had only pound notes, how should we set about the purchase of a paper, or pay for a bus ride, or buy a cup of tea?

One great difficulty in connection with money ought to be understood by anyone who can see the point of the following story:

A gang of counterfeiters turned out each week a great number of beautiful shillings, florins and half-crowns. They had agents in box offices of cinemas and theatres who distributed their silver coins to the public, and handed back to the criminals the genuine coins made at the mint. The fraud was discovered after a time; its success for a period was due to the excellent silver coinage which was illegally manufactured. It is only the Government, of course, which is entitled to manufacture such money as this.

The criminals were in the habit of paying into banks the genuine silver coins paid into the box offices by the public; but their own silver coins were just as good as the true ones. They were made in practically the same way, and contained just the same quantities of genuine silver. Why, then, did the gang of counterfeiters trouble to break the law by manufacturing such excellent silver coins?

The answer to this leads us to a question which is of very great importance to foreign traders. It is only gold which, throughout the world, is worth just as much in the form of metal bars as it is in the form of coins. When gold coins of full weight are melted down, the unstamped metal is worth just as much as it was in the form of golden sovereigns or half-sovereigns. But it is only gold which is standard money of this kind. The metal which is used for small change is cheaper. A shilling, for example, contains only a few pennyworths of silver, and a penny when melted down is almost worthless. Silver and copper coins form what is called the token coinage.

We are becoming more and more used to the idea of money which is not directly linked with gold: money, in fact, is becoming more and more what we call credit. Think of a bank-cheque: it is merely an order to pay. Two men, *A* and *B*, may have accounts at the same bank. When a cheque is presented at the bank there is no need for money to move at all. Mr *A* wishes to pay Mr *B*, by means of a cheque, a debt of £50; all that happens at the bank is that Mr *A*'s account is debited to the extent of £50, while Mr *B*'s account is credited to that amount.

The use of money is a sort of invention, and the government of a country always to a great extent controls this particular matter. A government may say at any time: "Just as our token coins are not really worth their face value in gold, so our paper money is in future going to be more independent of gold. We shall print just as much paper money as will help the exchange of goods most; but we do not promise to exchange it for gold on demand."

This may work very well with the home trade, but the level of prices for the foreign trade may be more disturbed. A foreign trader may answer, "Your token coins are not worth their full face value to us, and your paper money now seems to us a sort of token

Fig. 10

money. We do not know exactly what it is worth. It is only a gold coinage that means, at present, the same thing throughout the trading world."

This may be true, but after all, what is money? It is as it does: it is mainly a help in buying and selling. So it may well be a good thing to try to improve the system of money payments from time to time. The monetary system, as we have seen, has grown and changed to meet new needs; its changes are not likely to be ended yet.

QUESTIONS AND EXERCISES

1. Find out for yourself the chief ways in which money is transmitted from place to place by the Post Office.

2. "We are buyers of sovereigns, and in consequence of the premium ruling on gold we can pay much more than their ordinary value." What is the meaning of this advertisement?

3. Explain as fully as you can the meaning of the following statement: "Money is as money does". In your answer show the use of as many different forms of English money as you can. Make it clear that money is mainly a help in buying and selling.

4. What objections would there be to using as money in England at the present time, (*a*) silver coins only, (*b*) gold coins only, (*c*) iron and copper coins only, (*d*) paper money only, (*e*) diamonds?

5. Which of the following workers earns the larger total income:

(*a*) A mill-worker who has to support herself on 30*s.* a week, or

(*b*) A domestic servant who is paid £40 a year wages, with board, lodging and laundry free?

6. "Whoso hath sixpence is sovereign (to the length of sixpence) over all men; commands cooks to feed him, philosophers to teach him, kings to mount guard over him—to the length of sixpence" (CARLYLE).

Show how you would be sovereign over all men, if you had the chance, to the length of £20.

CHAPTER VII

MARKETS, PRICES, AND FOREIGN TRADE

By means of the money of which we have been thinking the values of marketable goods are measured. This process of measuring value in a market is followed by buying and selling.

We understand a market to be a place where traders meet to exchange goods or services. Servants, for example, may be hired at a market; and at other markets farmers offer for sale such things as poultry and butter, eggs, fruit, and vegetables. In return for this produce country people obtain from their market town boots and furniture, clothes, machines, and other goods made in city factories. In all the transactions it is through money that goods can be valued, and then exchanged.

In one market there is one price for the same article. By price we mean the money value of anything —the amount of money for which it can be exchanged. Thus those who possess buying power satisfy their wants: these lucky people have both the desire to possess something and the power to purchase it. Their demand is said to be effective. The demand of a beggar for a fashionable suit of clothes is not effective: he has no buying power: there is no supply for him. By the supply of something we mean the amount of it which is produced and is for sale, i.e. supply means the quantity of some commodity offered at a given price in the market.

The town market where country people do business with traders of a city is not hard to understand. But there are much wider markets than these. Whenever offers of goods and demands for them come together we have a market; and the offers and demands may come from the very ends of the earth. There is, as a matter of fact, a world market for many goods. Wherever goods are bought and sold there is a market, and the price at which the exchange takes place is the market price. Thus Liverpool is a world market for cotton, and London for wool. Many of the reasons for this we have already learnt. We have seen the home trade growing in England when the inhabitants of out-of-the-way settlements like Old Sarum were moving to the main roads. Smiths had to visit the fairs of the growing market towns for their iron ore, and the craftsmen of the new Salisbury worked in the woollen cloth industry. Foreign trade was developing. Wines were being imported more and more from Bordeaux, and wool began to come to Salisbury from Flanders.

We understand already that there are, as a rule, very clear reasons to be found for an industry growing in one place rather than another. It is a fair exercise in Geography to search for these reasons for the production of certain goods in particular places. It is not by accident that the cotton industry has developed in Lancashire. Liverpool became a great port for sound reasons. It is admitted at once that certain special advantages have led to the growth of towns like Leeds, Chicago and St Louis. We accept, then, as a beginning, the truth that industries settle, as a rule, where con-

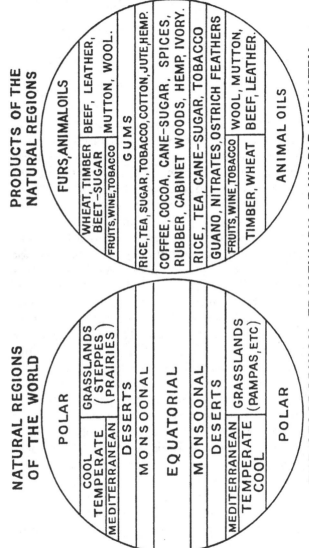

PRODUCTS OF THE
NATURAL REGIONS

FURS, ANIMAL OILS

BEEF, LEATHER,
MUTTON, WOOL.

WHEAT, TIMBER
BEET–SUGAR

FRUITS, WINE, TOBACCO

GUMS

RICE, TEA, SUGAR, TOBACCO, COTTON, JUTE, HEMP.

COFFEE, COCOA, CANE–SUGAR, SPICES,
RUBBER, CABINET WOODS, HEMP, IVORY.

RICE, TEA, CANE–SUGAR, TOBACCO

GUANO, NITRATES, OSTRICH FEATHERS

FRUITS, WINE, TOBACCO

WOOL, MUTTON,
BEEF, LEATHER,

TIMBER, WHEAT

ANIMAL OILS

NATURAL REGIONS
OF THE WORLD

POLAR

GRASSLANDS
(STEPPES
PRAIRIES)

COOL
TEMPERATE

MEDITERRANEAN

DESERTS

MONSOONAL

EQUATORIAL

MONSOONAL

DESERTS

MEDITERRANEAN

TEMPERATE
COOL

GRASSLANDS
(PAMPAS, ETC)

POLAR

THE GEOGRAPHICAL FRAMEWORK OF WORLD INDUSTRY

Fig. II

ditions suit them. It is, for example, all to the good that the labour connected with the production of our tea, cotton, sugar, coffee, and bananas should be performed overseas in those countries where sun and soil give so much freely to the worker. For nature is generous to us in other ways. In our own country there are large deposits of coal and iron. Our countrymen have invented much wonderful machinery, and they are very skilful in using it. Workers overseas often obtain what we call raw materials for manufacture more easily than we ourselves could produce them; and many kinds of food, as we have seen, are produced more cheaply abroad than in England. It is then surely a good arrangement which permits British traders to pay by means of such a commodity as cotton cloth for the products of tropical countries. We offer workers overseas goods like machinery and coal, hardware and boots to satisfy the wants of their people; they send us in return such commodities as corn and wool, cotton and fruits, rubber, tea and oil. It is simply another example of division of labour, of industries flourishing in places specially suitable for them.

One group of workers in our own country is engaged in making machinery, another group is heaving coal, others are growing corn. It is merely a sort of sequel to our story when we say that another band of toilers is growing tea in India, while others are producing wine in France. Then all interchange their products by means of home or foreign trade.

But this free interchange of goods and services, which seems so natural, is nothing but a dream of economists. In reality the obstacles to such a free flow are very great indeed. Import duties called tariffs are imposed at practically all ports, for all sorts of reasons. At present the terrible menace of unemployment is with us. One would think that all men and women would best find employment through the freedom of trade. But what is to happen if one group refuses the services of another overseas by heavy taxation of certain goods at the ports? The tariff wall of America may lead to unemployment in England. Through the awful wars of the past, nations are inclined to try to produce all their own requirements. People are more and more reluctant to rely for essential goods and services on others who may become their national enemies. Taxation in our times is very heavy indeed; it is tempting to collect money easily at the ports. Not long ago every child born in this country soon became either a little Free Trader or a little Protectionist. But the approach to the question of international trade is not now so easy as that.

In spite of all interference with the freedom of trade by means of tariffs, a vast amount of international commerce must continue. There is in existence a French petition which shows clearly that too much interference with natural activity may be absurd, even though particular traders may gain.

It seems a very serious document, but in reality it is a huge joke. One may read quite a lot of it, however, before the hoax is seen.

The petition claims to have been brought forward by the French candle-makers in the middle of the nineteenth century, and is thus described:

"Petition of the manufacturers of candles, wax-

lights, lamps, candlesticks, street-lamps, snuffers, ex-
tinguishers, and of the producers of oil, tallow, resin,
alcohol, and generally of everything connected with
light."

We may note in passing what progress has been
made since this petition was produced : our gas and
electricity have routed the ancient candle.

The petition proceeds :

"To Messieurs the Members of the Chamber of
Deputies.

Gentlemen,

We are suffering from the competition
of a foreign rival, apparently placed in a condition so
far superior to ours for the production of light, that
he absolutely floods our national market with it at a
very low price indeed. The moment he shows himself
our trade leaves us—all consumers apply to him ; and
a branch of native industry is at once done to death.
This rival, who is no other than the sun, wages war
to the knife against us, and we suspect that he has
been raised up to injure us by our trade rival England ;
for he does not dump his goods so freely in that cloudy
country. The Englishman is allowed to enjoy his
darkness, his mists, and his fogs.

What we pray for is that it may please you to pass
a law ordering the shutting up of all windows, sky-
lights, dormer windows, outside and inside shutters,
curtains, and blinds—in a word, of all openings, holes,
chinks, clefts and fissures, by or through which the
light of the sun has managed to enter houses, and

has, in the process, dealt a deadly blow at the trades which we represent. In our unequal struggle against a terrible competitor we appeal to our government to protect us.

We urge the following reasons in support of our request.

First, if you shut up as much as possible all access to natural light, and create a demand for artificial light, which of our French manufacturers will not be encouraged by it?

If more tallow is consumed, then there must be more oxen and sheep. Shall we not then see a great increase in our pastures, meat, wool, hides, and above all, manure, the source of all the good crops of our farms? If more oil is consumed, then the poppy and the olive will flourish. These rich plants will grow all the better because of the manure which will result, as we have shown, from the increased use of tallow. Our open spaces will be covered with resinous trees. Numerous swarms of bees will, on the mountains, gather scented treasures which are now, like the flowers from which they come, wasting their sweetness on the desert air. There is, in fact, no department of the work of our rural population which will not thrive vigorously if our request is granted.

All this is as true of the sea as of the land. Thousands of vessels will proceed to the whale fishery; and in a short time we shall possess a glorious navy, which will be a delight to the patriotic candle-makers and others who are now addressing you.

But what can we not say of the manufacture of gildings, bronzes, and crystals. They will shine forth in candlesticks and in lamps. Only think, gentlemen, and you will agree that all, from the wealthy coal-owner to the humble vendor of lucifer matches, will benefit by the success of our petition. If you confer upon us the monopoly of furnishing light during the day, first of all we shall purchase quantities of tallow, coals, oils, resinous substances, wax, alcohol—besides silver, iron, bronze, and crystal—to carry on our manufacture; and then we, and those who furnish us with such commodities, having become rich, will consume a great deal, and impart prosperity to all the other branches of our national industry.

In answer to our claims and arguments, you are only able to say that the light of the sun is a free gift of nature, and that to reject such gifts is to reject wealth."

So ends the petition; and although it was never meant seriously, it teaches us much in the matter of arguing a case in Economics. The tragic fact remains, however, that in almost every great town can be found unemployed men who would gladly work at any task which would be rewarded with buying power. When such men see goods produced abroad for sale in England, they say very naturally, "Could not our fellow-citizens so arrange matters as to permit us to satisfy their wants, in return for the buying power which at present we are without?"

This is a fair question, and in every case it must be fully answered.

Of course one may interfere with trade too much. Mistakes may be made by such interference. On the other hand, we now see more clearly that it may be a mistake not to interfere. It depends on the article. Put the case that we notice in our main shopping street, foreign boots, shoes, typewriters, linoleum, potatoes, wheat and oranges. Shall we impose a tariff to keep out, or to make dearer, any of these goods? It may or may not be good policy to impose a tax at the ports on some of these commodities and not on others. In any case, work must be done on the problem. Are the potatoes new? Can we produce good typewriters? Is there any chance for the industry to improve if for a time at any rate the market is not flooded with the foreign product?

"But," it may be said, "why include oranges?" Why not? There might be an English substitute, *e.g.* apples. An examination of the question of the supply of oranges will give us practice for arguing about the others. The case of oranges is rather easy; but the kind of argument is always the same.

Just imagine for a moment unemployed Scots urging the following case: "We beg to offer our services in connection with the supply of oranges, in return for buying power commensurate with our efforts and expenses. Coal must be mined, glass-houses must be erected, orange plants must be imported and tended, and artificial heat and our labour will then enable us to satisfy your needs."

Most expensive and inferior oranges might thus be obtained from Scotland. Natives of Seville have an unanswerable claim to supply this demand. Here is their case:

"All that artificial heat and manufactured equipment

can do in Scotland—and much more—the heat of the sun and natural growth produce in Spain. Much less buying power will recompense us for our easy task, and the oranges which we shall be able to offer at a cheap price will be in every way superior to those which our Scottish rivals can put upon the market."

We readily agree that in this extreme case it would be absurd if we were not allowed in this country to obtain any benefit from the sunshine of Spain. If the Seville orange prevents a possible Scottish rival from appearing on the world market, it is because natural and free heat does for the one much more than artificial and expensive heat does for the other. We can add other advantages to the Spanish industry in oranges: the soil is suitable and the labour is skilled. The knowledge and experience of the past workers has become a customary part of the training of Spanish peasants.

French wines may be cited once more to help to explain international trade. The government of the United States of America does not believe that those who make wine are usefully employed, and at present, in 1932, wine is excluded by law from the United States. When the people of Iceland wished to exclude such drinks, the wine-producing countries threatened to prohibit the importation of fish from the seas near Iceland.

A rather different case is shown when we think of the present superiority of the Japanese in all that relates to the manufacture of natural silk. It is so marked in our time that our workmen are almost prepared to admit that, in competing with the Japanese in this manufacture, they have met their masters. But it is not altogether easy to see why the Englishman should give up the struggle. The silk manufacture was not introduced into England yesterday, and much beautiful work by means of intricate silk machines and skilful craftsmen has been done, and is being done, among us. It might well be argued that some improvement in skill and speed could be obtained by our workmen in a few years if Japanese wares for a time at least could be heavily taxed at the ports.

In this and in other ways the government of a country sometimes tries to build up and encourage or protect an industry.

QUESTIONS AND EXERCISES

1. The orange is really a native of China. It was introduced into Southern Portugal and Spain after Vasco da Gama (1498) had discovered the sea-way to the East. Could a protective tariff be used to encourage its cultivation in our country?

2. Explain the meaning of the sayings: (a) "Trade follows the flag," (b) "Trade follows the telephone."

3. Do you know the present retail price of milk per quart? Ought the price to be different, (a) in summer and winter, (b) in the country and in the town, (c) for large and small quantities, (d) for bottled milk?

4. Discuss along the same lines the cost of a ton of coal, dealing with the season, the place, and the quality and quantity of the coal purchased.

5. "Buyers are builders. Buy British." What does this advertisement mean?

6. (*a*) Why have our countrymen become the great sea-carriers of marketable goods? (*b*) How many types of vessels engaged in shipping do you know? (*c*) Write a list of all the occupations you can think of that are directly connected with shipping.

CHAPTER VIII

WAREHOUSES, OFFICES, AND BANKS

The shops and shoppers have taught us much. Now come stories from warehouses, offices, and banks.

The wholesale trader must be an expert in buying and selling. Of course he must either have a lot of money of his own or be able to control the capital of others. He must buy in bulk from the makers of goods, and sell to the retailers in small quantities, just as articles are required to meet the demands in the retail shops. His warehouses must be well situated as regards transport, *i.e.* he must, as a rule, keep his stock of goods near a railway station or even near a sea-route. Both the delivery of his stock from the manufacturers and their packing and forwarding to his own customers depend on transport. A wholesale dealer must be able to judge in advance what the retailers will want from him; so he has to study all markets and prices. He is often a world merchant, with his own ships and foreign agents. Some wholesale firms deal in almost every class of goods, while others limit their buying and selling to a particular market.

Let us now peep into a typical wholesale warehouse. It is situated near the railway junction. We understand that there is no need for a wholesale warehouse to be near its customers if it is able to obtain supplies and forward them. From this warehouse traders from all over the country obtain by rail their supplies of provisions like rice, butter and coffee. It is a firm of the world merchants of whom we have spoken: its branches and agents are found in many countries, buying from farmers and planters. They even possess ships of their own to transport their goods. With regard to butter this business house has an inland wholesale trade, for it collects butter from farmers at home, in addition to importing part of the supply from abroad. Having thus collected tea, rice, butter, coffee, and so forth, from all parts of the globe, its job is to sell to the retailer. It should be mentioned that this particular wholesale house grows some tea in its own plantations in Ceylon.

The firm has been very successful, and its great profits have been due, to a great extent, to its general manager, and his buyers and salesmen. The general manager is the captain of the ship; he guides it to the happiest seas. Or we may say he is the specialist who is consulted first when all is not well with the great business; for he has his fingers on the very pulse of trade. He knows all about the markets of the present, and much about past years. But in addition to this he should be either a prophet or the son of a prophet. It is his great job to know what the retail shopkeepers will want to buy from him in the near future. The buyers, salesmen, and commercial travellers are also very skilled workers: they have between them reduced the buying and selling of goods to a fine art. A retail shopkeeper may choose to visit the warehouse himself, and see a wide selection of marketable articles. In that simple way he may see his future stock before he buys in the wholesale market. If a retail tradesman cannot visit the warehouse he must wait for the next call of the commercial traveller. The latter is sometimes called

the outside salesman, or he is said to be "on the road."
A trader often makes use of both methods of buying.

The advertising department of the office is generally
near the section occupied by the buyers and salesmen.
Advertising is just as important to the retailer as to the
wholesaler; in fact, at first it seems more important
in the retail shop, for artistic and striking window-
dressing is a retailer's job. But a manufacturer or a

WHOLESALE WORLD TRADE WORKERS

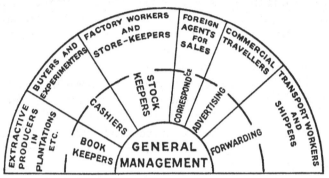

Fig. 12

wholesale dealer may advertise his goods throughout
the length and breadth of the land; and then the public
simply compels the retail shopkeeper to purchase them.

Advertising, however, means much more than window-
dressing. Wonderful and striking posters have to be
prepared or selected for the hoardings. Slogans, such
as "Buy British," "Eat more fruit," and so forth, have
to be thought out. The advertising section of this office,
in short, is composed of specialists. They sometimes
call themselves publicity agents. They know much

better than the rest of us whether the hoardings—the poor man's picture galleries—are likely to help sales more than space in magazines and newspapers. They know whether the design of a poster will attract public attention or not. They know how to draw up an advertisement for the newspapers, and what type to use. We like to see their coupons for free samples in newspapers. We like them to advise the firm to distribute freely sample goods without payment, or to recommend from time to time sales in certain lines at half the usual price. The electric signs in all colours in all towns are the masterpieces as yet of the advertising departments. Perhaps, however, we should give pride of place to trade exhibitions and pageants.

The business seems very efficient; everything seems a model of good arrangement. The cashiers and book-keepers are housed very near each other, for frequent consultations between them seem to be necessary. The documents for goods shipped or otherwise forwarded are dealt with by the invoicing department near at hand. The secretary can tell us all that is to be known of the quantities and qualities of the stocks, the date of their receipt, and their source of origin. We can guess what is being done by the busy writers in the goods inward department.

We agree, then, that the office of a successful commercial company is a hive of industry. Salesmen, advertisers, travellers, and clerks, pass quickly from one office to another for advice and information. Typists and packers maintain a steady buzzing in the mail department. Accountants, cashiers, typists, and ledger clerks are as common as office furniture.

It is a great and loyal team that we have seen playing the business game. There is practically always a fine spirit shown by all workmen in a great commercial house; for each knows the value of his fellow-workers, and that the lonely furrow he would plough alone would be a desolate failure.

They know that on the brain and energy of their chief the success of the business depends most. He forms the most important link with the outside world. He is responsible for the whole organization.

The salesmen readily admit that they can offer a good article at a fair price only if the buyers of the firm are experts in the changes of values. The profits of whole businesses depend on whether the buyers understand world markets or not.

Not even the stock-keepers should be passed by without honourable mention. The goods must be so arranged that they can be readily controlled and checked. The examination of the stocks, their cleanliness, and their preservation, are important tasks. If this work is well done, its general fitness strikes one at once. The temperature of the warehouse must be suitable, its lighting must be good, there must be an entire absence of every kind of vermin, and every device that aids the best storage of food must be employed. In this department immense losses may be the result of inattention to duty.

Finally there is the red ensign. Not all wholesale merchants own their own ships. Perhaps we should do well to visit a firm of special standing in the shipping industry. Some of its great ocean steamers will bring raw materials for our manufacturers, and carry back

our finished products. Among these big ships, however, must be included the ocean greyhounds which
carry mainly passengers and mails. There are also short
voyage steamers and tramps. The liner has a fixed
route, but the tramp has no fixed line, and was formerly
termed a "seeker."

It is difficult to keep pace with the progress of our
whirling age. Once it seemed much for a business
man to make use of telegraph, telephone, and cable.
It is a plain fact that in our times the aeroplane must
be seriously reckoned with in the business of transport
of goods as well as passengers. It is equally true that
radio stations are beginning to play a considerable
part in spreading trade information. The Empire
broadcasting station is intended partly for this very
purpose.

Another hive of business industry that we should
certainly try to enter for a moment is an Insurance
Office. We already know in a vague kind of way that
if ships are wrecked, or if goods are destroyed by fire,
an insurance company will indemnify any trader who
has paid the necessary premium. It is through the
risks of commerce that insurance thrives.

What does insurance really mean? Although a commercial enterprise undertaken by a group of workers
who have the control of capital, there are deeply-rooted
ideas of kindness and humanity in insurance. The risk
of bad fortune is met by a system of mutual support.
Through the money paid in the form of premiums,
a merchant is no longer compelled to keep a great
amount of capital unemployed. Without a system of
insurance every trader would have to keep idle a large

sum of money to meet such a run of bad luck as drove Antonio into the toils of Shylock.

Let us marshal our facts in order. Money is paid into the insurance companies in the form of premiums, and in return, the company undertakes to pay to the insurer a much larger sum upon the happening of a certain contingency. This reads like an extract from the prospectus of an insurance company, and one or more of them can easily be obtained and read. So vigorous is the insurance business that the difficulty for most of us is not to obtain these documents, but to avoid them.

Their advertisements are as disturbing as those for patent medicines. "Do you know how many more years of life you may expect?" they ask in large print. That is only the introduction to the alarming risks they know of. We remember the famous advertisement of one company: a car containing 29 laughing men is shown falling over a precipice. There is one passenger, however, who is not giggling like the rest: he is the only one whose life is not insured.

While the chief branches of the business of insurance are life, fire, marine and accident, we may also be guarded by this business group against burglary, sickness, loss of employment, and many other risks.

It is strange to be told that an employer may insure against any theft on the part of clerks, travellers, collectors, and so forth. A farmer may even insure against the risks of bad crops, and accidents to his animals, while a tradesman may insure against bad debts.

In one of these offices we might see someone at work on the figures which enable him to state what premium should be paid to meet this or that risk. He must have all the latest figures relating to the particular chance he is trying to reckon. Thus the most recent statistics dealing with Life Insurance have led to a reduction in the premiums which must be paid in this department; for the expectation of life is now longer than it was formerly. One worker may have to advise on the rates of insurance to be paid by a trader for the safe transport of goods overland through various countries. This official will actually be able to say not only which countries have more thieves than their proper share, but also the lands where honesty is flourishing, and where decaying. Another may need to be an expert in all that relates to the construction of ships; for it may be his duty to state what premium should be demanded to insure this or that vessel. He may also have to insure a ship for a particular voyage: he should then know what the risks of one sea are in comparison with another.

Finally, we will call at a bank. In a general way we may say that the work of a banker is to receive money from people who have no particular use for it at the time, and to place it at the service of suitable business men.

Money, then, is saved by thrifty people and is lent to a banker, who pays Interest on it. As a rule, very small amounts may now be paid into a bank. More Interest can be allowed if the money is not to be withdrawn for a definite time, for then it can be used in more ways in business. Money is then said to be lent on deposit; if the money can be withdrawn at any time the account is current. The rules of the Post Office

Savings Bank are rather different. Anyone can easily learn all about them by opening a small account.

Money is withdrawn from a bank by means of cheques. Every depositor buys a cheque-book, which contains stamped printed forms. These are used to instruct the banker to pay this amount or that to the person named in the cheque. It is not very hard to persuade the proud possessor of a cheque-book to show it to others. The Post Office Savings Bank does not make much use of cheques. The work of the banker is to lend money safely at a higher rate of Interest than he pays for it. Thus his profits are made.

The banker is really a sort of pawnbroker; or shall we say, the pawnbroker is a sort of banker. A captain of industry might say to a banker, in one of the private rooms behind the counter, "I have just bought a valuable site for a boot and shoe factory. Here are the legal title-deeds. You will find that they are quite in order. How much can I borrow on them?" What the manufacturer means is that he needs a loan of capital for his business, and the title-deeds of the site are offered as security. Unless the manufacturer can repay the loan capital at the agreed time, what is called the security can, by the agreement, be sold for ready money.

Yes, it certainly reminds us a little of the three balls! For something pledged and retained on certain conditions, ready money is supplied to people in straits. A watch is the best known security of the pawnbroker.

But banking has not the dismal associations of pawnbroking. No discredit whatever is connected with loans from a banker: it is rather a matter of credit. The banker has to decide whether the would-be borrower ought to be credited. Is his business scheme sound, or is it not?

If the banker lends more than the actual value of the title-deeds, he will have to ask all sorts of questions about the proposed boot factory. He will be blamed

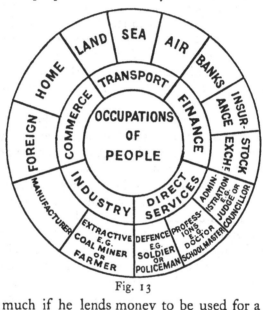

Fig. 13

very much if he lends money to be used for a wild-cat scheme.

Glance on leaving at the work proceeding in the bank outside the private rooms. Thrifty tradesmen enter in a steady procession, some carrying bags of money, like the bees returning to the hive with their honey. Cashiers receive their deposits at the counters, while clerks quickly hand them their pass-books, which contain full statements as to their accounts.

QUESTIONS AND EXERCISES

1. Show how world trade gains through improvements in communications and transport.

2. Would you rather be engaged in (1) forestry, (2) office-work, or (3) engineering? Describe in as much detail as you can the day's work you would like to do.

3. Select any business of which you have some special knowledge, and describe the work done by the most highly paid men in it. Then describe the work done by some of the workmen whose wages are low.

4. If you were the publicity agent for a firm of wholesale world merchants trading in tea, how would you advertise new blends recommended by the tea-taster?

5. Is your house insured against fire? Are you insured against burglary? Do you agree with this? Give any other examples of insurance that you know of.

6. Write down all you know about a cheque. Think out the details of a transaction in which a bank manager assists a trader. As part of the imaginary business show how a cheque is used.

7. Do you think that advertisements by means of posters on public hoardings are more effective than insertions in newspapers? Write a list of advertising posters now showing in what appears to you to be their order of merit.

8. Describe any trade pageant or exhibition that you have seen.

CHAPTER IX

INCOMES

Such is the machinery which delivers the goods for the shop-windows. In the main, it is admirable. Its results are wonderful. But what of the machinery which removes these goods from the shops to individuals? This is not nearly so satisfactory. It creaks rather badly at times, and needs a large supply of lubricating oil.

What shall we say, then, of the way in which goods leave the shops, and the people to whom they are sent? These lucky buyers must have money to spend: what really decides how much people shall get for themselves? We have at length reached the question of Wages, Profits, Rent, and Interest. The young economist will find this a very difficult subject. It is more refreshing altogether, before plunging into it, to think for a moment of the Greek victors at the Olympic games being rewarded with sprays of laurel.

In a general way we know that wages are earned because employers expect to make a profit out of the work for which they are paid. We quickly understand that people will not work for nothing, and that land cannot be had for nothing. At first sight Rent, Wages, and Profits seem easier to understand than Interest. A great French economist used to tell the following simple story to explain why Interest is paid.

"There was once in a small town," he said, "a poor carpenter who worked hard from morning till night.

One day the workman, whom we will call James, thought to himself, 'By means of my hatchet, saw, and hammer, I can make only coarse furniture. Thus my wages remain very poor in spite of my hard work. I need more capital to help me. For example, if I had a plane, I should please my customers more, and should be able to earn more money. Well, I will make myself a plane, and see if I prosper more.'

"Ten days later James had made a very fine plane which speedily revealed his good calculation, for his trade rapidly increased. He was beginning to reckon how much money he would make by his plane when his friend William, a carpenter in the neighbouring village, said to him, 'You must give me a helping hand; lend me your plane for a year.' James was rather angry. 'How can you ask me such a favour!' he said, 'but if I grant it, what return will you make to me for it?' 'Nothing,' answered William, 'don't you know that Interest should not be paid?' 'I know nothing of the kind,' said James, 'but I do know that if I lent you my plane for a year, it would be like giving it to you. Do you think that is why I made it?' 'Very well,' said William, 'I admit that when I wish to borrow your plane I am asking you to do me a service. Now, what do you ask from me in return?' 'First,' said James, 'when the plane is worn out, you must make another exactly like it.' 'That is perfectly just,' agreed William, 'I submit to the condition. I think you must be satisfied with this and can require nothing further.' 'But I think otherwise,' said James sharply, 'I made the plane for myself, and not for you. I expected to gain some slight advantage from it. I made the plane with the idea of improving my output through its help, and naturally hoped to gain better pay through my better work. When you return a plane to me in a year, you will have gained all the profit for which I hoped. Why should you expect me to do you such a service? It is most unreasonable! Now you may have the use of my plane on these conditions. Besides the restoration already bargained for, you must give me a new piece of wood each year as a compensation for the advantages of which I shall be deprived.'

"These terms were agreed to, and very strange does it seem that at the end of the year when the plane came once more into James' possession he lent it again on the same terms. The supply of wood which he thus obtained was enough to enable him to make other tools, some of which he lent to others in accordance with the bargain made with William."

What is the inner teaching of this little story? In the first place the discussion between James and William becomes somewhat heated, and almost approaches a quarrel. Team-work and general helping agreement we have seen everywhere in the work of the world: co-operation of toilers in all lands has been shown. But when the hunters have joined almost merrily in the chase, when they have called to the aid of man the swiftness of the horse and hound, and when at length they have won together the spoils of victory, trouble has always arisen in the end. It is not easy to see how to divide the reward.

At any rate, we may agree that James, the French carpenter, gave as clear an explanation as possible why William, his fellow-worker, ought to pay him Interest on borrowed capital. William agreed, although somewhat sulkily: he was, at any rate, glad to borrow capital from James again and again, and to pay him Interest.

Let us think of an example a little more like the business of to-day as we hear of it, and the Commercial

INTEREST IS A PAYMENT FOR—

ALLOWING ANOTHER FOR THE TIME BEING ONE'S PROPERTY TO ENJOY THE USE OF

CONNECTED WITH THE INVESTMENT OF MONEY THE WORK

THE RISK OF THE LOSS OF THE CAPITAL INVESTED

Fig. 14

Arithmetic as we know it at school. Why, then, should a shopkeeper who borrows £100 for a year have to pay back not £100 only but £104 or £105, or more or less.

Interest is paid for the use of a certain amount of capital for a certain length of time. What would happen if the rate thus paid were very low, say, $1°/_°$.

This would not make much difference to the savings of very rich people. The small number among us who possess an enormous amount of wealth can hardly spend it all on themselves. But most people who save a certain amount of money could spend much more for their own personal benefit at once if they wanted. As a rule, when money is saved, thrifty people hand over to bankers their claim on that part of the stock of goods which they might consume but do not. Others obtain these savings from the bankers, and the goods are then consumed in some form of productive labour. If the rate of Interest paid were as low as $1°/_o$, these ordinary savers would spend more on themselves. Capital to lend would then become scarcer, and its value would rise—just as we shall see that the value of labour and land increases through their scarcity. Sometimes new inventions make it necessary to replace old machines quicker than usual. For reasons of this kind the demand for capital will increase, and its price will rise.

Dividing the spoils of victory among the hunters, those who own the horses and dogs, and those who own the ground covered by the hunt, is a very hard job. People do not really go hunting for ready-made coats, but workers all the same have to be paid for making them. And how much? What is the worth of the work of one toiler compared with another? An inquiry was made some little time ago into the manufacture of ready-made coats in New York. At that time the making of such a coat was divided into thirty-nine distinct processes. One man would do nothing from morning till night, and from year in to year out, but make pockets. It was the life-work of another to press sleeves. There was another of this group whose job was to cut button-holes; his neighbour was a button-hole marker; another was a button marker; there was a button-hole sewer, and so on. To make a shoe in some factories it required a hundred and seventy-three operations, each performed by a group of labourers with a special name.

At the time of which we are speaking, however, the most dazzling example of the subdivision of labour was furnished by the manufacture of a fine watch. Here machines, power, and men were at work together. As regards human labour there were at that time a surprising number of workmen, each using a different kind of machine.

It is very well to be told by an employer of labour that a man gets as much for his work as he is worth. The question we have to answer is this: why is one man's work worth more than another's?

A farm labourer is really a very skilful craftsman in comparison with a button-hole cutter; so is a fisherman, with his wonderful collection of knowledge and skill in sailing, fishing, and all that relates to the weather. Is there any system by which these differences of ability are taken into account in the fixing of the wages of these workers?

We have already said that wages are paid because the employers who pay them expect to make profits out of the work for which the wages are paid. But we must learn a little more about this. All young economists are interested in wages.

Take the motor-car industry. The profits of an

employer will depend on the price he can get for each car, so a workman's wages will be better when trade is good than when it is bad. We know that Trade Unions give assistance to workmen in bargaining with employers; but money cannot be shared by anybody unless it has first been gained for sharing. When cars are being sold in great numbers, profits ought to be good, and higher wages can be paid.

We should notice another point. If one manufacturer buys the very best machines for his workmen to use, the finished article will be all the better because of the splendid equipment of the factory or works. Hence an up-to-date employer is able to pay his workmen better wages through making full use of capital. When a workman is making something with the help of a machine, there is no one alive who can say just exactly how much of the final product of the work is due to the man and how much to the machine. The man's work gains in every way if he uses the best machines, and his wages become larger. With the best equipment there will be the best finished product for the market, and the best profits. For the finest cars there will be a good demand, profits will increase, and wages will increase also.

Think of some particular workman—a dustman, for example. A dustman is an excellent and necessary member of our society, but his wages cannot be increased much by the use of capital, or the demand of the public for his goods. If few people were born poor, and if there was no supply of dustmen, wages for collecting garbage would have to be high to attract men to such an unpleasant calling. But very poor labouring families are very common, and, as a rule, the ordinary poor children cannot be trained to be skilled engineers, or apprenticed to any skilled trade. The poorest children must become labourers, unless they are very clever; and the wages of the labourers remain low because there are so many of them. If these poor people have any chance whatever, they should try to train their children to be skilled artisans, or brain-workers of some kind. The supply of brain-workers and skilled artisans is much smaller than that of manual labourers, for their training for their work is longer and more expensive. The supply being thus limited, their price, or wage, is a high one.

Think of our doctor once more, but this time in connection with what we say he is worth to those who pay him. What shall we say of his special ability? Think of his examinations and education. What of the length and cost of his training? What of the capital of which he makes use? What of the demand for his services? The answers to these questions explain why the doctor is paid more than a miner or a dock labourer.

We sympathize very much with the good and useful worker who hews coal far underground, often lying in a most uncomfortable position almost in the dark. Low wages and bad conditions seem often to go together.

A thought may be given to other depressed workers. There is the child labourer in the East, there is the poverty-stricken Indian peasant, there is the Chinese coolie: all these workers are almost beggars. Yet from people like these we often get the raw materials for

our manufactures. Since all the agents for the production of wealth have been fitted together so cun-
ningly, our country has become richer and richer.
The standard of life has risen for practically all our
countrymen: leisure and comfort are shared to a
greater extent than formerly among all.

We must now think a little more carefully about
profits. What are the profits of a shoemaker? What
are his wages? We should find it hard to tell one from
the other.

We have noticed already how water is supplied to
a large city. What are the profits to be obtained for
this service?

We have seen how much capital is necessary to
secure a water supply. The long story began with the
thirsty man living near a river who made a bucket
and then hollowed out logs for a wooden conduit.
This led us to think about the great amount of capital
used at the present time to dam up rivers, to pump
water, to store it in cisterns and transport it in pipes.
The profits obtained through this service would chiefly
be the Interest to be allowed for use of the capital.

A butcher's profits, on the other hand, would have
to pay his wages, and to meet many other expenses.
There would have to be a payment for the use of a
motor-car, a shop, and its equipment. The butcher,
in hot weather particularly, runs the risk of losing a
lot of money from time to time; and some profits
have to be counted on to meet a possible loss. They
might pay for a sort of insurance. Profits thus seem
to mean all kinds of payments. What we should
really do is to consult some precise man of business

who knows exactly what he means by profits, and can show what they amount to from his books. The term "gross profits" ought to be used to mean the excess of receipts over expenses in any business. Wages, risk of loss, and other expenses must be subtracted from these gross profits, and then net profits will remain.

The share of the income from industry which is paid for the use of land is called rent. The land for which it is paid may be a valuable city site, or a stretch of beautiful pasture land, or a rich orchard, or a cornfield. In the state in which it offers most help in business, land is not often a free gift of nature. Lumber may have been cleared away from its surface, swampy districts may have been drained, dry soils may have been irrigated. Sometimes roads have had to be made to connect the particular land with villages and markets; buildings may have been constructed for the use of cattle, wells may have been sunk, expensive scientific manures may have been applied to poor soils, and hedges and ditches may have been made. These are all very necessary services, and payment must be allowed for them.

There is not enough good and suitable land to satisfy all who want the use of it. There is, then, a bidding among those people against one another for it. They have to pay a price for it because the supply is limited.

It works out something like this. A stretch of land may be used by a farmer to produce wheat, clover, beans, or potatoes. But the rent paid for the use of the land by a farmer will be less than that offered by a railway company for a section to be used for works, stations, and permanent way. Another grade of rent for land would be received from a business man who used it as a site for factories or engineering works or shops. In these cases boots, clothes, cars and aeroplanes would be a sort of crop from the land.

Thus the uses made of land may change. It may be farmed in a more skilful way than formerly, or a sky-scraper may replace a bungalow on it. Still, its actual quantity cannot be increased to any great extent. We have seen rich rewards going to the scarcer forms of labour; and we can now note the same principle at work with regard to the payment of rent. When land is desired for more than one purpose, the higher payment of rent decides to what use it shall be put. The railway may pay more than the factory, the factory sometimes more than the shop, and the shop more than the farm.

In considering the prices paid for goods and services, we find that we have to think often of competition. We know a good deal already about sports' competitions, and now we see the same sort of struggle going on around wages and prices. In the past, competition of this kind led to much harshness; the losers lost too much; the consolation prizes were very few and very poor. But some forms of competition seem a cheerful part of life. Think of the competition in a hunting party: horn and bugle replace voices; dogs and horses take the place of men and of one another. Each is striving with might and main for a place.

"All around us we see this competition to render service. As man harnesses the powers of nature in his service, they struggle among themselves. The winds of the sailing-ship are dispensed with as regards that particular job when the steamer goes down to the sea. The coal of the steamship fights a losing battle with oil. The rich virgin soils of America are substitutes for much English cornland. The charcoal of the forests is replaced by the coal of the depths.

WAGES LABOUR INTEREST CAPITAL

AGENTS OF
PRODUCTION
···AND···
THEIR
REWARDS

ORGANISATION PROFITS LAND RENT

Fig. 15

Everywhere there is competition. The pictures move. The optical toy in which we may see an endless variety of forms is called a kaleidoscope. The forms of the things used by men to help in the production of wealth may then be described as kaleidoscopic.

"But the keenest encounters are between men and machines; and the story of the struggle is a rough one. The wonderful Jacquard machine appears late

in the chronicle of the silk industry. In the market-
place at Lyons this machine was once publicly burnt;
but Jacquard's bronze statue is one of the sights of
the city."

At the beginning of this hard chapter we rested for
a moment on our rather parching road of Economics,
and were tempted sorely to loiter in more flowery
places. Luckily the laurel decorations won by the
ancient Greeks at the Olympic games, to which we
referred, suggest a sort of holiday trade to show the
part often played by competition in fixing prices and
wages. Let us consider the business of the practical
sports' outfitter. "We supply," he proudly announces,
"all requisites for tennis, cricket, croquet, football,
golf, badminton, hockey, lacrosse, fives, swimming,
boxing, fencing, and all indoor and outdoor games."
We must imagine that the demand for the stocks in
the retail shops has been suddenly increased. Something like a revolution in the world of sport has
occurred: the enormous crowds of spectators at all
matches have decided to play a little themselves
instead of merely watching, talking, or betting. The
cricket crowd is buying tickets no longer, but is purchasing bats, balls, nets, bags, stumps, and sundries.
The former spectators stand in queues in the shops.
The increased demand is effective enough, for everybody in every queue is well supplied with buying
power. The tennis pavilions are similarly deserted,
and the demand for rackets is immense. Most unlikely
people are detected with badminton shuttlecocks in
their possession, and golf balls are entangled with all
the other pocket furniture. A popular newspaper has

transformed the possible football crowds of next season into teams, and the manufacture of balls, clothes, and boots for them is regarded as a wise anticipation of demand. "Flannelled fools," "muddied oafs," large gloomy men in plus-fours, and graceful hockey players seem to be the most eager purchasers of the outfits necessary for their various games. It is plain that the demand for requisites for sports far exceeds the supply. Prices will now rise. More buying power must be given for the goods for which the demand is so great that the supply cannot cope with it. Some of the people in the queues must now leave them because of the increased prices. The demand, then, is not quite so great as it was; for not all the old customers can pay the higher prices.

The demand may be less than it has been, but it is still so great that it remains unsatisfied to a great extent. Prices of sports' equipment remain high, and the profits of the business firms connected with all phases of sports' outfitting are excellent. A high rate of Interest can be paid to induce people to invest money in the industry, the rents paid for shops and factories employed can be raised after a time, and the wages earned become larger. Now try to imagine what workers in other trades think of these high wages. What will they try to do? In palmy conditions such as these, who would not be a sports' outfitter? For what occupation will people try to train their children? Investors with money to lend will note the high rate of Interest offered by manufacturers of sports' requisites. Capital and labour will, of course, flow in larger quantities to this flourishing business.

There will be more workers, more raw materials will be purchased, additional factories will be built, more shops will be rented; and after a time the new supply will overtake the demand. Prices will then fall somewhat, and Profits, Interest, Rent and Wages will be paid by the industry at the usual rates.

That is what we mean by saying that through competition a certain level of prices tends more or less to be maintained.

Competition is a good servant, but a bad master. Harsh competition grinds the faces of the weak; but the story of monopolies in our school histories shows how useful competition may be sometimes. The subject of monopolies, however, is much too difficult for the young economist—particularly after a chapter like this.

QUESTIONS AND EXERCISES

1. Do you think that a postman engaged in the delivery of letters will as a rule earn more or less than a skilled engineer? Give your reasons.

2. Describe as fully as you can some industry in which you believe that the high wages paid to workmen are partly due to the specially good equipment of the works.

3. Why do film stars obtain such enormous incomes? Write down a list of other classes of people with huge incomes, and try to account for them.

4. Is money well spent when gambling tickets are bought with it? Does a lucky gambler really earn the wealth which he receives? Who really pays him his winnings?

5. Many more shops are being opened even in towns where the number of people is not increasing. Can you think of any reasons for this?

6. Refer to advertisements in newspapers for the terms on which certain goods may be obtained on the hire-purchase system. Write out as long a list as you can of articles that may be purchased in this way. Show how interest is paid to the traders as part of the instalments.

7. Why is a worker usually paid at a higher rate of wages for overtime? If the hours of labour are reduced from 8 to 7, will the output of work always fall in the same proportion? Show what you mean by referring to homework given to pupils by school teachers.

CHAPTER X

TAXATION AND WISE SPENDING

A budget really means a sack and its contents—a sort of bundle, a collection of things. Every year the Chancellor of the Exchequer makes a statement to the House of Commons, in which he deals with all the odds and ends that have to do with the collection and spending of the taxes. A private person also sometimes arranges in an ordered statement his own expenses.

We have said much about the getting of money. What we are now to think about is how money is spent, and how it ought to be spent. What are the things that we buy? What are the things that we ought to buy? There is a well-known phrase about getting value for money. That is our last subject.

A few family budgets would help. What is wanted is an exact record of how a week's wage is actually used. Many young economists can obtain a record of that kind. They can thus begin real economic research for themselves. How much money is spent on food? How much on rent? How much on amusements? Some money, let us hope, is saved.

Very likely no amount of money paid away in the form of taxation would appear in many family budgets. Still, such an item should always be included. How is this?

Any society like the nation into which a man is born must have rules for the common good. Some important duties the government of a country is always bound to perform. An army, a navy, an air force, and a police force must be maintained. What about the machinery of the Post Office? Money, weights, and measures must be controlled by Parliament. There are the law courts, parks, and roads. Some of these public interests, *e.g.* education, health, and public assistance, are controlled to some extent by county and town councils or other local authorities. The national government, with King and Parliament, is described as central. From it local authority radiates.

It would be lucky if we were thinking about taxation on the day when the annual statement with regard to taxes and supplies was being made in Parliament. Soon after the end of every March, this national budget appears in all the newspapers. From this one can soon decide, among other matters, whether any family budget can properly omit an item for taxation.

The Post Office has already been mentioned. Part of its work is to carry letters. One pays for a stamp to be affixed to a letter, which the government thereupon becomes responsible for carrying. Does one pay a tax when buying a stamp? No! for a tax is a payment which one is compelled to make to the government, quite apart from the particular use to which the money will be put. A tax is paid when a dog license is bought; for the money is collected to be spent in any manner authorized by Parliament.

Taxes are either direct or indirect. A direct tax is collected from the person who is really intended to pay it. The Income Tax is a good example of such a tax.

An indirect tax is different. It is collected from one

person while another must, in the long run, pay it. Some taxes of this kind are bound to reach every family in the land.

Thus, when tobacco enters the country, the importers pay a tax on it; but when they charge their customers more for their tobacco because of the tax, they really transfer the payment to the smokers. The indirect tax is thus shifted from one person to another.

The government tries to make its system of taxation fair. The well-to-do pay at a higher rate than the poor, and the very rich at a higher rate than the well-to-do. This is seen very clearly in the case of the Income Tax. Every penny matters to a poor man.

The money which the local councils are permitted by Parliament to control is obtained partly from the central government of the country and partly from rates. The latter are charges imposed by the local authorities upon the occupiers of property.

Rates might well be included among the troubles of our early friend, the small shopkeeper. This trades-man might oblige us by explaining whether he manages to make his customers pay part of his rates in the form of increased prices. The best opportunity to find out exactly how rates are spent is to read the details printed on the demand note sent to each house. A sort of local budget is thus revealed.

Young people will notice with interest the item for expenses connected with the police force. This is a pay-ment shared by the national and local authorities. It reminds one of the tremendous sums of money spent by the nation on the maintenance and equipment of forces for defence against criminals at home and possible enemies abroad. Our feelings towards our gallant defenders are cordial. But these splendid fellows would themselves admit that the crushing burden of armaments is a grim menace to prosperity; and its apparent necessity at present is a sad thing. In this matter, however, we do not sorrow as they that have no hope.

The money borrowed in the past, mainly for wars, has helped us to the freedom that we enjoy; but the National Debt, honourable to those who borrowed and to those who lent for victory, is nevertheless a burden under which we stagger.

Mankind lives in movement, and the movement should be forward; that is what we call progress. Money should be spent in such a way that the changes that must come may be for the better, and that remedies may be found for great evils.

There is now always with us, for example, the grim menace of unemployment. People become unemployed now in great numbers through no fault of their own, and this unemployment continues for long and depressing periods. Some payments from public funds thus become the due of the worthy unemployed.

On the other hand our country contains more people able to enjoy more of the comforts of life than ever before. The products of the whole world are now on our markets. The houses, food, clothing, conditions of work, and amusements of the man in the street are better than in former days. And we still have hope. The best is yet to be. The golden age is before us.

No one would now be found to deny that it is right for a certain amount of public money to be paid for the relief of the poor. This is an ancient problem, and our history books have much to say about it. Closely connected with it are the expenses incurred in regard to Public Health. We all agree that money spent in purchasing health is properly used. Parks, open spaces, playgrounds, and the medical service of the Insurance Acts come into this story. The present position in which the hospitals find themselves supplies us with a very useful exercise. We all admit that their blessed work must be continued and extended; and yet we all know how very hard it seems to be to maintain them by means of voluntary contributions. Can wealth be better used than in supporting institutions such as these?

Two main points remain to be stressed. In the first place, all public accounts should be very public indeed. It should be easy for everyone to find out exactly how all rates and taxes are spent; and special and independent auditors should be required to investigate all public expenditure. The government auditor does this for the local authorities. When highway accounts were first brought under audit, it was found that some money collected from the people to pay for roads had been spent on wedding presents, some on presentation portraits, and some on visits to theatres. As a general rule, however, our public finance is a model for the whole world.

The next point to emphasize is that before a citizen can usefully control the spending either of his own or public money he must have prepared himself for the task. He must have thought much about the proper use of wealth.

What should we value most? In struggling for wealth of one kind, is it possible to lose something more valuable? Labour is subdivided to gain wealth which may be bought and sold. But something is lost in the process. "It is not, truly speaking," wrote John Ruskin, "the labour that is divided, but the men— divided into mere segmentary men—broken into small fragments and crumbs of life, so that all the little piece of intelligence that is left in a man is not enough to make a pin or a nail, but exhausts itself in making the point of a pin or the head of a nail."

The best answer we can make to this is that, through this division of labour, the increased wealth may be used to buy beautiful things for the workers. Thus their leisure and recreation may be passed in elevated and refined pursuits. Some wealth should always be used to support the nobler arts:

"I want to know a butcher paints," sang Browning,
"A baker rhymes for his pursuit,
Candlestick-maker much acquaints
His soul with song, or, haply mute,
Blows out his brains upon the flute."

By using wealth for these human arts, a man, when he leaves his work behind him, may cease to be part of a soulless machine. Thus may all know what William Morris was so anxious to teach them. By the proper use of wealth all should share in a common culture. All should know of the ancient stories and the mighty dead. All should honour the wisdom of the wise, and love the poetry of the race, even though this or that disciple may aid in the production

of wealth only by working on the heel of a boot. We
may by wise spending all enjoy in common,

"The painter's hand of wonder;
    And the marvellous fiddle bow,
And the banded choirs of music;
    All those that do and know.
For these shall be ours and all men's,
    Nor shall any lack a share
Of the toil and the gain of living
    In the days when the world grows fair."

Thought and teaching of this kind are bringing us
all nearer together. There must be a struggle for life,
but it is not waged to the bitter end. A spirit of modera-
tion is abroad.

"For more and more it is becoming clearer that those
who struggle are men with the same joys and the same
sorrows. To them all the big things—the great things
that really decide all deep human happiness and suffering—are much alike. God and the world, birth and
death, youth and age, love and friendship, fidelity and
treachery, health and sickness, all mean the same
thing—for example, to employers and employed. It
is so easy to lose one's sense of proportion. In these
big things of life and death men are more equal than
in the small things. Any difference as to wages, for
example, is but a small affair compared with what we have
noted above. Of course the competition between man
and man may be harsh, but it should not be unneces-
sarily bitter. It is an impersonal thing. It is like the
competition between a spade and a plough. It springs
from no man's desire, but arises out of the nature of

the things that shape our ends. Some clashing of opinion and interest is to be regarded as natural, just as a thunder-storm is natural. Thus men should expect opposition, it may be that they should oppose, but they should always respect the man in the opponent."

These thoughts were uttered by a great German thinker. His message to his fellow-men was this: "See, we struggle, we are separated by different views and feelings; but your hair, like mine, is showing locks of grey."

The great hope of human happiness in the future is that these finer feelings will make a more powerful appeal to the coming generations. They have been uttered often by great leaders, but in the past the majority of men have not given heed to them. Yet a man whose soul is not deeply stirred by noble thoughts is without the larger part of human nature.

QUESTIONS AND EXERCISES

1. Do you think that roads ought to be controlled by private owners, and paid for by a system of tolls? Ought the private owners of motor coaches plying for hire to make a special payment for the wear and tear of the roads?

2. Write out full details of the family budget of any weekly wage-earner.

3. What is your favourite recreation? Show why you think it is preferable to some others.

4. (a) Write a list of as many taxes as you can that are paid by various members of your family and their friends.

(b) Do you think any particular tax in your list is a bad one? Give your reasons.

5. How are hospitals supported? Is the present system quite satisfactory? Can you think of a better?

6. (*a*) Describe any carnival in support of charities that you have seen. Have you ever taken part in one?

(*b*) What other methods have you observed by which money is raised by private subscription in support of good causes?

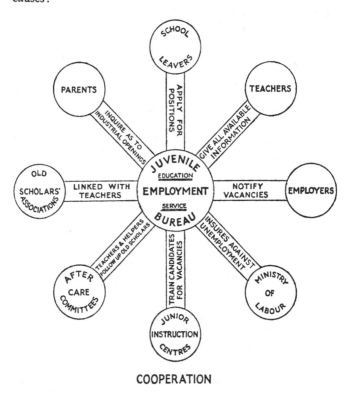

COOPERATION

Fig. 16

INDEX